Editors

Eric Migliaccio

Michelle Combs

Managing Editor

Ina Massler Levin, M.A.

Editor-in-Chief

Sharon Coan, M.S. Ed.

Illustrator

Howard Chaney

Cover Artist

Denice Adorno

Art Coordinator

Denice Adorno

Imaging

James Edward Grace

Rosa C. See

Product Manager

Phil Garcia

Publishers

Rachelle Cracchiolo, M.S. Ed.

Mary Dupuy Smith, M.S. Ed.

W9-CFJ-538

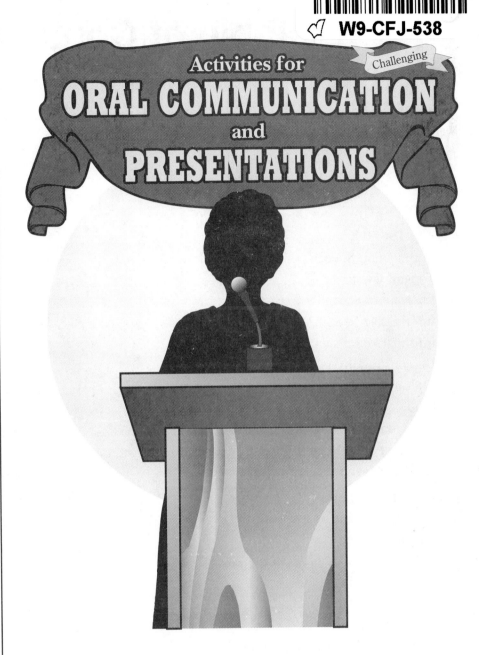

Activities for
ORAL COMMUNICATION
and
PRESENTATIONS

Challenging

Author

Beverly Baxter, M.S. Ed.

Teacher Created Materials, Inc.

6421 Industry Way

Westminster, CA 92683

www.teachercreated.com

ISBN-0-7430-3085-1

©2001 Teacher Created Materials, Inc.

Made in U.S.A.

Table of Contents

Introduction

Activities for Oral Communication and Presentations offers a series of activities to introduce students to a wide variety of methods and uses of oral communication. In essence, this book is an invitation to play. Beginning at a very young age, children use play to explore different lifestyles. For instance, they may role play being a fireman or a bride—even "playing house" falls under this category of exploration. It is this attitude of play that allows children to develop new skills and explore new avenues that will become integral to their lives. In much the same way that the game of "dress up" allows children to try on new looks, this book provides children a chance to try on new ideas.

This book is divided into three major parts of oral communication:

☞ Public Speaking

Students will explore various types of public speaking and gain experience in a variety of activities.

☞ Persuasive Speech

Students will learn the art of persuasion in our society: exploring discussion, the campaign speech, the commercial, problem solving, role playing, labor negotiation, conflict resolution, and debate.

☞ Drama

Students will participate in creative dramatics, improvisation, pantomime, oral interpretation of prose and poetry, reader's theater, and melodrama.

Use this book to enrich your classroom lessons. The materials are not limited to speech and oral communication classes, but are appropriate for youth and civic groups, party and ice-breaker ideas, staff development training sessions, or family gatherings. Use these ideas or add additional materials of your own to explore the art of oral communication.

These activities utilize the guidelines set as criteria for developing a good lesson. It has been suggested an effective lesson adheres to the following guidelines:

I. Introduction (20% of class time)
- A. Concept is introduced.
- B. Standards and benchmarks are set.
- C. Emotional hook or teaser to tempt the student into the learning process is provided.

II. Content (65% of class time)
- A. Teacher input (20%)
- B. Students actively participate (45%)

III. Evaluation (15% of class time)
- A. Student success is identified.
- B. Further instruction and exploration is planned.

Studies show the amount of learning that actually occurs from the following activities:

lectures—5%	audio visuals—20%	practice by doing—75%
reading—10%	demonstration—30%	teaching others—90%
	group discussion—50%	

Standards

Definition: A curricular standard is a general statement of what a student should know and be able to do in academic subjects.

Part 1

○ Listen and speak effectively for a variety of purposes (e.g., to follow directions, obtain and provide information, gain clarity of speech, organization and outlining skills, media presentations, questioning and interviewing skills).

○ Organize and deliver planned and impromptu oral presentations; use language and technology appropriate to knowledge and purpose.

○ Communicate effectively and use acquired skills in job interviews and leadership roles.

○ Demonstrate accuracy in articulation and enunciation.

○ Demonstrate knowledge and skills in research, outlining, and organization.

Part 2

○ Listen and speak effectively for persuasion for a variety of purposes (e.g., to promote products, ideas, problem solving techniques, conflict resolution, discussion, and debate) in informal and formal situations.

Part 3

○ Listen, perform, and entertain for a variety of purposes (e.g., pantomime, oral interpretation, storytelling, creative dramatics, improvisation, readers' theater, and melodrama).

○ Demonstrate knowledge in performance and entertainment skills in pantomime, oral interpretation, and storytelling.

○ Demonstrate knowledge in performance and acting skills in creative dramatics, improvisation, readers' theater, and melodrama.

Delivery

Definition: Delivery is simply a combination of all the speaking skills used to convey ideas or communicate with the listeners.

These are the skills to develop to improve your delivery:

○ Relax! Most people experience stage fright when they stand and speak in front of a group. Breathe deeply and speak slowly to avoid a quivering or breathless voice.

○ Stand with one foot in front of the other and weight balanced to avoid that feeling of shaking and trembling. If your hands shake, hold them in front of you, rest them on the podium, or let them hang at your sides.

○ Concentrate on what you're saying, and the stage fright will pass.

○ Don't rush through your speech and speak too rapidly. Take your time and say each word distinctly.

○ Put notes on a large card or a page saver. This will help steady them if you tremble and will help you look calm. (An outline form is included on the next page.)

○ Don't read your speech from notes. Use an outline and talk to the listener. If the group is frightening, concentrate on one person at a time.

○ Vary the rate, pitch, volume, intensity, and rhythm of your voice. This is called vocal inflection.

○ Some movement for emphasis or to give you a relaxed look is good, but don't move back and forth or develop nervous mannerisms. Avoid wringing hands, tugging at clothing, or twisting hair.

○ Gestures are simply moving your hands to emphasize a point. It is good to talk with your hands, but plan small, relaxed gestures.

○ Diction should be clear and easily understood. Clip consonants and move lips to enunciate. Slow speech patterns down and don't run words and phrases together.

○ Grammar and vocabulary should be practiced ahead of time to avoid problems.

○ Avoid fill-in phrases, such as "you know," "aaa," "um," and "you see."

○ A mistake is a normal part of any learning experience. If you make one, correct it and go on.

○ Speaking is acting. Act like you are having a great time and your listeners will believe you.

Organization

The best method of organizing a speech is the three-point outline. It enables the speaker to tell at a glance exactly what point he or she is making. It is the road map for the speech. If you get confused, it steers you back on course.

I. Introduction and Attention Step

Use a joke, anecdote, or story as an attention step. It is also good to state your topic.

II. Body (all basic content of the speech)

A. First Subpoint

    1. Description

    2. Provide details and supporting information.

B. Second Subpoint

    1. Description

    2. Provide details and supporting information.

C. Third Subpoint

    1. Description

    2. Provide details and supporting information.

III. Conclusion

Refer back to the attention step and tie it all together.

Outline Form

I. Introduction

II. Body

A. Supporting Detail	
B. Supporting Detail	
C. Supporting Detail	

III. Conclusion

Critique Sheets

Many of the lessons in this book contain critique sheets. These exercises in evaluation serve the dual purpose of providing feedback to speakers and training the listener to look for certain elements that create effective communication. Please complete these exercises for each student by observing these key elements:

◆ Be kind and constructive—encourage the speaker.

◆ If there are tips that have helped your skills, share them on the critique.

◆ Avoid mean-spirited, cruel, or rude comments.

◆ If you notice distracting mannerisms or any area to correct, write that on the comments portion of the appropriate section.

◆ If one area is a strength, share that with the speaker. We never tire of hearing positive comments, especially when we are completing a difficult task. Please elaborate in the comments section.

◆ Circle a rating in each area. The ratings are as follows:

Rating	Description	Meaning
1	Superior	The speaker made an outstanding effort.
2	Excellent	Very pleasing effect—even if a problem or two are noted.
3	Good	A good effort was made and ideas are communicated.
4	Fair	This rating means this area needs improvement. If this number is circled, improvement must be listed on the comment section.

Remember, the speakers you evaluate will also evaluate you!

Introduction Speech

The introduction speech provides the opportunity for the beginning speaker to present a well planned speech that is easily prepared. It provides the class with a chance to become better acquainted. This speech is informal in style and may be communicative and spontaneous. This style allows the first speech to be less rehearsed and encourages the speaker to genuinely communicate rather than simply read to the audience.

The interview time may be one class period to prepare and serves as an ice breaker for a new class. Students who have been well acquainted will enjoy hearing classmate responses to the personal inventory. This is a very simple way to organize and present the first speech.

Presentation Time: 3 to 5 minutes.

Assignment: Select a partner and complete the personal inventory on page 10 by interviewing each other. This information will be used to introduce the partner to the class. If the number is uneven, create a three-member team. Each person introduces someone else; students should not introduce themselves.

Introduction

Plan your introduction ahead of time (use the space provided on page 11) and write the introduction in the provided space. A good introduction is an attention step or teaser that addresses the content of the speech. It is always a good idea to begin with a joke or anecdote (an amusing or entertaining incident from the subject's life). Humor is fine, but it is also interesting to provide a serious or life-changing incident that provides insight into the personality of the subject. (Note: It is never good—or even acceptable—in any speech, to use humor or joke at someone's expense! This is cruel and tasteless, and it reflects poorly on the speaker! It is the goal of this assignment to enhance and uplift the person.)

Conclusion

This is a time to summarize and conclude the speech. It is usually a good idea to refer to the introduction after the summary to conclude and provide closure. Every speech should have a definite conclusion. Example: "As I shared with you at the beginning, Jane's earliest memory was a fire in the family home. That fire has seemed to light a spark that has inspired great accomplishments in her life. We can only look forward to great achievements in her future." Use the space provided on page 11 to write out your conclusion.

Student Reflection Page

After presenting your speech, complete the student reflection page (page 11).

Introduction Speech (cont.)

Personal Inventory

Select a partner in the class and answer the following questions. Then, use your interview information to introduce your partner to the class. Use the space provided on page 11 to plan your introduction and conclusion.

1. Birthplace _____

2. Places person has lived _____

3. If the house were on fire, one thing (other than people, pets, or photos) I would save would be

   _____

   _____

4. The location where I would like to live is _____

5. If I won a trip, I would visit _____

6. If I could go to dinner with anyone famous (living or dead), it would be _____

7. If I could change the world, I would _____

   _____

8. In ten years, I would like to be working as a(n) _____

9. The symbol I'd select to represent me is _____

10. If I were a car, I would be a _____

11. My favorite food is _____

12. My birthday is _____

13. I am most thankful for _____

14. My favorite color is _____

15. I become very upset when I see _____

    _____

16. The political issue or person I would like to never hear about again is _____

    _____

17. The time period I would travel to is _____

18. My favorite charity is _____

19. The thing I most like about America is _____

    _____

    _____

Introduction Speech *(cont.)*

Student Reflection

Introduction to speech: _____

_____

_____

_____

_____

Conclusion to speech: _____

_____

_____

_____

_____

1. What thoughts gave me confidence?_____

   _____

2. What were my physical reactions to fear? _____

   _____

3. How did I feel when the speech was over? _____

   _____

4. How would I improve my speech? _____

   _____

5. Were my notes easy to handle?_____

   _____

6. Was I able to make eye contact? _____

   _____

7. Did I repeat unnecessary words or phrases? _____

   _____

8. How did the listeners respond to my speech? _____

   _____

Tongue Twisters

The most important part of communication is to be heard and understood. Good diction is an important skill for good speakers.

Tongue twisters are a fun way to practice good speech techniques. It is impossible to say a tongue twister without concentrating and using your mouth and lips to communicate difficult phrases. Practice these tongue twisters. Repeat them three times each.

- ◯ Big, black, baby buggy bumpers burned rubber.

- ◯ Charlie Chaplain chews Chinese chow.

- ◯ Ride a red wagon, raving "Woo, woo, woo!"

- ◯ Shaggy Shirley sheared several sheep in the sheep shed.

- ◯ Peter patrolled the planet packing pop guns.

- ◯ Zip! Pow! Zoozer zapped a zinger.

- ◯ Moping Molly melted moist marshmallows.

- ◯ Six sharp, shifty sharks shooshed a school of shrimp.

- ◯ Polly Pitcher pitched plump plums.

- ◯ Proud pumpkins ponder pitiful perils.

- ◯ The shells she sells are surely seashells.

- ◯ Eight gray geese grew greedy over gravy.

- ◯ Big Bill blew big blue bubbles.

- ◯ "Swim, Sam, swim!" shrieked his six scared sisters.

- ◯ The shady chef served cheap sheep soup.

- ◯ Five fearful frogs fled from fifty fierce fish.

- ◯ The big book crook took the big cookbook.

- ◯ The rain ricocheted off Ruth's wet, red roof.

- ◯ The black back brake broke.

Tongue Twisters *(cont.)*

Some tongue twisters ask questions:

○ How much wood would a woodchuck chuck if a woodchuck could chuck wood?

○ How high would a horse fly if a horsefly would fly high?

○ How much dew would a dew drop drop if a dew drop did drop dew?

○ Which witch watched which watch?

○ On a light night, do you need a nightlight?

○ Did the butterfly flutter by the butterfly?

○ Is there a spider inside the cider beside her?

○ Do crickets chirp in thickets?

○ Do busy buzzing bumblebees buzz busily?

○ Did a skunk sit on a stump?

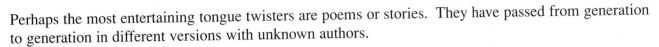

Perhaps the most entertaining tongue twisters are poems or stories. They have passed from generation to generation in different versions with unknown authors.

A canner exceedingly canny
One morning remarked to his granny
"A canner can can
Anything that he can,
But a canner can't can a can, can he?"

A skunk sat on a stump.
The skunk thunk the stump stunk,
But the stump thunk the skunk stunk.

Theophilus Thistle, the successful thistle sifter, while sifting a sieve of unsifted thistles, thrust thirty thistles through the thick of his thumb. Now, if Theophilus Thistle, the successful thistle sifter, thrust those thistles through the thick of his thumb, how many thistles did Theophilus thrust through the thick of his thumb?

Spoonerisms

Another form of tangled storytelling that closely resembles the tongue twister is the *spoonerism*. These are most easily identified with actor Andy Griffith. Many people have delighted in his spoonerism, "The Pee Little Thrigs." To create your own spoonerism, simply read a familiar story, mixing initial consonants and blends with other words in the phrase, such as "The Three Little Pigs."

Assignment: On a separate piece of paper, create your own tongue twisters or spoonerisms and read them to the class.

Impromptu Speech

The impromptu speech is an unprepared speech that one gives with spontaneity. It is often done when the speaker draws a topic—sometimes a silly one—and gives the speech off the top of his or her head. Each member of the class can supply one topic to put into the drawing. If preferred, the class may base their speeches on the topics suggested on page 15.

A speaker may prepare an impromptu speech by following the basic three-point speaker outline:

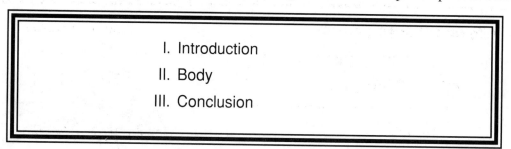

I. Introduction
II. Body
III. Conclusion

Introduction

The introduction may be an attention-getting statement, joke, or anecdote. It is always a good idea for speakers to learn famous or well-known quotations, since these make great introductions. It is also possible to present a simple incident in a dramatic or storytelling format.

Example: "A young child rummages through the garbage behind a grocery store. She pulls her thin jacket around her frail body and shivers against the cold. For her, this subject—hunger in America—is a harsh reality."

This introduction has accomplished several goals:

- gotten the attention of the listener

- personalized the subject

- created sympathy for a presented need

- provided an organizational tool to restate the need and develop a conclusion.

Conclusion

When presenting a conclusion, refer back to the introduction.

Example: "Feeding the hungry may hold little interest for the comfortable, but, to the child rummaging through garbage for provisions, it is of immediate interest today—and has an even graver impact on her tomorrows."

Impromptu Speech *(cont.)*

Presentation Time: 1 to 3 minutes

Assignment: After choosing a topic, each student should give a short impromptu speech on the subject. Topics for impromptu speeches may be provided by the class. However, if preferred, you may cut out the following suggestions for topics, place them in a hat, and have each member draw one out for his or her speech.

Life on Other Planets	Favorite Sport
Watermelon	Bubble Gum
Pizza	Favorite President
Most Memorable Character	Elephants
Coping with My Sibling(s)	The Best Pet to Have
Most Memorable Day	Favorite Day of the Year
First Day of School	Marshmallows
Mistakes I've Made	The Best Way to Get Exercise
News Story I'm Tired of	How to Make Lots of Money
A Memorable Book	What Makes Me Really Mad
A Memorable Movie	If I Could Invent a Candy
How to Improve School	How to Promote World Peace
Favorite Actor	What Food I'm Best at Cooking
Funniest Person Alive	The Best Car to Own
Favorite TV Show	The Best City to Live In

Impromptu Speech *(cont.)*

Critique Sheet

Speaker: _____

Evaluator: _____

Circle an evaluation mark in each category and add constructive comments in the provided space.

1—Superior   2—Excellent   3—Good   4—Fair

Delivery Technique:

Facial Expression (relaxed, animated, and responsive):	1 2 3 4
Vocal Expression (variance, rate, pitch, volume, intensity, inflection):	1 2 3 4
Diction, Grammar, and Word Usage (No "you know's," "um's," or "ah's"):	1 2 3 4
Eye Contact (looks at audience, not overly dependent on notes):	1 2 3 4
Bodily Action and Gestures (relaxed, comfortable stance, no distracting movements, notes handled well):	1 2 3 4

Comments: _____

_____

Organization and Content:

Introduction (attention step):	1 2 3 4
Body (followed organized outline and developed points):	1 2 3 4
Conclusion (summary and closing comments):	1 2 3 4

Comments: _____

_____

Informative Speech

The informative speech may be on any topic about which you are interested in learning more. The speech is just relating the facts on a selected researched subject. Topics should not be controversial in nature or opinion based. Topics may be simple like "the pencil sharpener" or complex like "the Civil War." Remember, if a broad topic is chosen it should still be a simple overview presented within the time limit. A note card or organizer may be used and the speech should adhere to the following three-point outline format:

  I. Introduction

 II. Body

III. Conclusion

The informative speech is research-based. An educated person does not know everything but *does* know where to look it up. Select a topic that interests you, and you will discover what fun research can become. Today we are the most information-rich society. Of course, the most promising place to research is the Internet, and it has become easily accessible. Most public libraries are now on the Internet and will be happy to teach you to research a particular subject.

If you select a topic, such as a particular community, you may reach the Chamber of Commerce or local newspaper through the Internet and request information. Don't overlook sources like the school library and the card catalogue. Information on both the Internet and the card catalogue may be accessed or referenced by subject. If your topic is hot air balloons, look under the topic. You may find a whole book or more on the subject in your school library. This is your chance to become an expert on a subject that interests you. Chances are that if it is of interest to you, it will also make an interesting and informative speech.

Presentation Time: 3 to 5 minutes

Assignment: The following is a list of topics to choose from. Select one (or choose your own) and develop your informative speech from your research.

- a book
- an artist
- a sport
- stamps
- videos
- flowers
- an animal
- dinosaurs
- computers

- hairstyles
- a music style
- a fashion designer
- a food or beverage
- a musical instrument
- a form of transportation
- an amusement-park ride
- the life of a famous person
- a community service organization

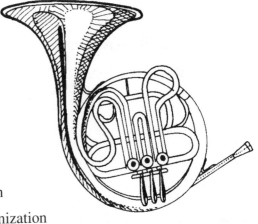

Informative Speech *(cont.)*

Critique Sheet

Speaker: _____

Evaluator: _____

Circle an evaluation mark in each category and add constructive comments in the provided space.

1—Superior 2—Excellent 3—Good 4—Fair

Delivery Technique:

Facial Expression (relaxed, animated, and responsive):	1	2	3	4
Vocal Expression (variance, rate, pitch, volume, intensity, inflection):	1	2	3	4
Diction, Grammar, and Word Usage (No "you know's," "um's," or "ah's"):	1	2	3	4
Eye Contact (looks at audience, not overly dependent on notes):	1	2	3	4
Bodily Action and Gestures (relaxed, comfortable stance, no distracting movements, notes handled well):	1	2	3	4

Comments: _____

Organization and Content:

Introduction (attention step):	1	2	3	4
Body (followed organized outline and developed points):	1	2	3	4
Conclusion (summary and closing comments):	1	2	3	4

Comments: _____

Informative Presentation

Talk Show

Presentation Time: 7 to 10 minutes

One way to convey information about a certain topic is to plan a presentation in the form of a talk show. Work in small groups to design a talk show with a famous host and guest experts. The show should have an introduction, main body, and conclusion just like an informative speech; yet different people will be discussing the different parts. For example, in place of a speech on volcanoes, the talk-show host could introduce a geologist to discuss the features of a volcano and how they are formed; a person who lived through a volcanic eruption could discuss the effects; and a volcanic scientist could discuss detection techniques for future eruptions.

You can also videotape your show or add special effects. If possible, dress up in costumes, utilize simple props, and use gestures and expressions appropriate for your characters.

Game Show

Presentation Time: 7 to 10 minutes

Another entertaining way to present information is in the format of a game show, such as *Jeopardy*! (There are many popular game shows for children today on TV. Discuss the formats of these shows to see which ones best lend themselves to presenting the information clearly.) Using this format, the game show host will introduce the players and the topic for the day. The categories for questions will be the main points the presentation is to cover. The players will play the game, revealing correct and incorrect information. Points will be awarded as on a real game show. At the end of the presentation, when all of the topics have been covered, a winner will be selected. The winner can then summarize the topics of the informative presentation, and the game show host can give a closing statement.

Informative Presentation *(cont.)*

Critique Sheet

Speaker: _____

Evaluator: _____

Circle an evaluation mark in each category and add constructive comments in the provided space.

1—Superior   2—Excellent   3—Good   4—Fair

Delivery Technique:

Facial Expression (relaxed, animated, and responsive):   1   2   3   4

Vocal Expression (variance, rate, pitch, volume, intensity, inflection):   1   2   3   4

Diction, Grammar, and Word Usage (No "you know's," "um's," or "ah's"):   1   2   3   4

Eye Contact (looks at audience, not overly dependent on notes):   1   2   3   4

Bodily Action and Gestures (relaxed, comfortable stance, no distracting movements, notes handled well):   1   2   3   4

Comments: _____

_____

Organization and Content:

Introduction (attention step):   1   2   3   4

Body (followed organized outline and developed points):   1   2   3   4

Conclusion (summary and closing comments):   1   2   3   4

Comments: _____

_____

Demonstration Speech

Presentation Time: 3 to 5 minutes

This is the speech type with which we are most familiar. It simply instructs us in step-by-step directions for performing a skill. In this age of the infomercial, we have all seen the products that have caused us to wonder how we ever lived without them. On this page, you will find a few ways to insure that your demonstration will be similarly successful to an infomercial. After you have studied these, look at the list of topics on page 22. Then select one from the list or create a topic of your own to give a demonstration speech.

1. Organize your materials ahead of time and make sure you have all the items you need. A storyboard will help your organization of different steps and cues.

1. Explain how to make French Toast.	2. Show various ingredients.	3.
4.	5.	6.

2. Practice the step-by-step action so that it will be automatic to you.

3. It is often a good idea to reveal ahead of time what you will do and then explain each step as you perform the skill.

4. Include every step, taking your time as you do so.

5. There may be long gaps as you wait to complete one step. For example, if you are making French toast in an electric skillet, explain different toppings and ways to serve the meal as you wait for the bread to brown.

6. Handle props or equipment with ease. If you need an electrical outlet, locate one before the speech so you won't be wandering around searching for it. The key to a relaxed demonstration speech is to prepare in advance!

Demonstration Speech *(cont.)*

Topics

Any skill you can show or demonstrate step by step and bring in appropriate props to actually perform the steps as you speak is a good topic. It is probably not a good idea to select something everyone can already do—like lacing and tying your shoes—unless you are speaking to a kindergarten class. The following are suggested topics to help in the selection process and preparation of your demonstration. Don't rule out a special interest you have, such as swimming or flying, just because you can't bring in the pool or the airport. With careful planning you may demonstrate different swim strokes and explain the process of teaching the skill of swimming. A pilot may also bring in a chart of an instrument panel and demonstrate the process of a takeoff or landing. Your listeners will enjoy hearing the steps involved in the acquisition of this specific skill. This is the process known as teaching, and we are all lifelong learners. If you don't have a particular skill to demonstrate, have someone teach you; then reteach the skill for your speech.

crafts	changing a tire
origami	puppet making
juggling	balloon animals
martial arts	giving manicures
needlepoint	blow drying hair
hair braiding	blowing bubbles
gift wrapping	carving pumpkins
ventriloquism	making silk flowers
pet grooming	creating a family tree
woodworking	playing an instrument
golf techniques	making paper airplanes

Demonstration Speech *(cont.)*

Organizer

Topic:_____

Outline	Props & Materials	Actions

Demonstration Speech *(cont.)*
Critique Sheet

Speaker: _____

Evaluator: _____

Circle an evaluation mark in each category and add constructive comments in the provided space.

1—Superior   2—Excellent   3—Good   4—Fair

Delivery Technique:

Facial Expression (relaxed, animated, and responsive):	1	2	3	4
Vocal Expression (variance, rate, pitch, volume, intensity and inflection):	1	2	3	4
Diction, Grammar, and Word Usage (no you knows, ums, or ahs):	1	2	3	4
Eye Contact (looks at audience, not overly dependent on notes);	1	2	3	4
Bodily Action and Gestures (relaxed, comfortable stance, no distracting movements, notes handled well):	1	2	3	4
Steps to Demonstration (planned and clearly demonstrated with props; materials handled without distractions):	1	2	3	4

Organization and Content:

Introduction (skill to be demonstrated explained):	1	2	3	4
Body (followed organized outline and developed points):	1	2	3	4
Conclusion (summary and closing comments):	1	2	3	4

Comments: _____

_____

_____

_____

Multimedia Presentations

Many of us are visual learners. This skill has been honed through movies, computers, and television. Today's technology allows us to enhance communication. Even before computers filled classrooms, speakers used visuals to enhance their presentations. For many years, teachers have used flannel boards to enrich a story. Tape players have been used to set a mood or provide special effects. The slide show has been very effective in illustrating ideas or taking people to places they have not been.

All of these techniques can now be programmed ahead of time into your computer systems. Technology is becoming a very helpful tool to communication. It is now possible to project to listeners images or ideas we only dreamed of a few years ago. We now even have the technology to project and discuss an individual's genetic code. The most effective presentations utilize a blend of technology. This presentation serves two main purposes:

1. To acquaint the speaker with the new technology being updated every day

2. To allow the speaker to develop skill at coordinating a multimedia presentation utilizing several technologies

The effectiveness of the multimedia presentation lies in the novelty, preparation, and poise developed in handling special effects. Charts and graphs may be handheld or they may be put into a computer slide show through the use of programs such as *HyperStudio* or *PowerPoint*. The slides may be developed through the use of a scanner on the computer. Family photographs, artwork, or even scripted information can be used. Then the programs allow you to put everything into a special slide show that may be projected on a screen in front of the room. The programs may be automatic or may be operated by the speaker at will. Special sound effects or musical background may also be used. The following pages will discuss other suggestions for presentations.

An opaque projector is also a great asset in this type of speech. It is possible to project magazine pictures, photographs, or even poetry script with these.

The technology of the previously mentioned programs even allows us to select a graphic or picture and animate it. This type of animation is often used in our weather forecasts, which, with their blend of graphics and animation, are great examples of multimedia presentations.

The multimedia presentation is used in churches, management meetings, faculty inservices, classrooms, and sales. It is also becoming a vital tool in the field of medicine. These skills are necessary in today's job market. Select a topic on the following pages you are interested in. It is also acceptable to create your own. If you are not certain how to present an idea, research and learn.

Multimedia Presentations *(cont.)*

Topics

These ideas should get you started, but remember that the effectiveness of the speech is in your ability to communicate, organize, and multi-task rather than how much technology you can employ. The visual aids or multimedia techniques should only enhance the presentation—and sometimes less is more.

Examine the sample organizer on page 28 for ideas on how to plot the steps involved in your multimedia presentation. Then use the organizer template on page 29 to plan your presentation.

○ Music buffs might record examples of different styles of music or rhythm and discuss each, using a tape recorder. You could also select one musician and play segments of his songs.

○ Select a topic such as color wheels and project those on a screen using an opaque projector. These projectors can also show personal artwork.

○ Tell a children's story and make your own pictures or illustrations. Copy them from a book and hold them or project them. If several pictures are used, it is good to use an easel for organization.

○ Select a famous or historical personality and review his or her life. Use pictures copied from magazines or books. It is also fine to use the book and illustrations as long as the group is small and each person may see them easily.

○ Use a VCR and show different dance styles in competition or a biographical sketch.

○ Use a flannel board and tell a children's story with illustrations.

○ Do a makeup presentation and show before and after pictures.

○ Describe different art styles and show examples by the pictures themselves or by projection.

○ Do a book report and use a chart on an easel that will enable you to write ideas about the book.

○ Prepare a presentation about fishing and show pictures of different types of fish. You may use songs about fishing as background music.

○ Give a speech about architectural styles of houses and show pictures of the houses or videotapes of ones in your hometown.

○ Develop a presentation of clothing styles of certain decades of the 20th century. Project pictures or slides of examples.

○ Prepare a presentation of flower types using a slide presentation. Use various short poems about flowers. Describe the plant and where it grows, etc.

Multimedia Presentations *(cont.)*

Topics *(cont.)*

○ Select a decade of the 20th century and play examples of the popular songs of the decade. You may also project pictures or present news events from that period. You could name it something like "You are There."

○ Present a speech informing the group that you have found life on another planet, but show familiar pictures of Earth. Example: Here is a picture of a religious icon they pray to several times a day. (Show various telephones). They even have shrines on the street where they stop to worship. (Show public phone booth). The group will conclude it is you that are an alien.

○ Show vacation slides or pictures in a slide show format.

○ Prepare a travelogue of your hometown, with pictures of sites of local interest.

○ Prepare a presentation about breeds of dogs, cats, or horses. Explain the differences between the breeds and where each originated.

○ Present various table-setting themes with pictures. There are books of these in local libraries, and contests are even held. Another interesting topic like this is quilts. There are wonderful pictures of quilt patterns and stories of the history involved with each.

○ Show costume designs and generate ideas about how to make them.

○ Present various wedding-dress styles or pictures of wedding cakes. These are easily obtained in bridal magazines.

○ Develop a presentation showing examples of classic cars and explain their backgrounds and histories. You might even use background music about cars.

Multimedia Presentations *(cont.)*

Sample Organizer

Topic: Snow in Literature

Outline	Visual Aids	Audio	Actions
I. Read Robert Frost's "Stopping By the Woods on a Snowy Evening"	*HyperStudio* program with projection of animated snowflakes	Recording of "Let It Snow."	None

II. Description
  A. Memories
  B. Snow themes
	Pictures of snow scenes (hand held)	None	Walk around with pictures

III. Conclusion Read "The First Snowfall" by J. R. Lowell	Continue animated snowflakes	None	None

     28

Multimedia Presentations *(cont.)*

Organizer Template

Topic: _____

Outline	Visual Aids	Audio	Actions

Multimedia Presentations *(cont.)*
Critique Sheet

Speaker: _____

Evaluator: _____

Circle an evaluation mark in each category and add constructive comments in the provided space.

1—Superior   2—Excellent   3—Good   4—Fair

Delivery Technique:

Facial Expression (relaxed, animated, and responsive):   1 2 3 4

Vocal Expression (variance, rate, pitch, volume, intensity, inflection):   1 2 3 4

Diction, Grammar, and Word Usage (No "you know's," "um's," or "ah's"):   1 2 3 4

Eye Contact (looks at audience, not overly dependent on notes):   1 2 3 4

Bodily Action and Gestures (relaxed, comfortable stance, no distracting movements, notes handled well):   1 2 3 4

Visual Aids/Media Helps (well prepared, handled and added to the overall effect):   1 2 3 4

Organization and Content:

Introduction (attention step):   1 2 3 4

Body (followed organized outline and developed points):   1 2 3 4

Conclusion (summary and closing comments):   1 2 3 4

Multimedia Effects (related to and enhanced presentation):

Comments: _____

Eulogies

Presentation Time: 5 to 10 minutes

A eulogy serves one simple purpose: to honor and praise a person's life or accomplishments. It differs from an obituary, which lists only facts. A good eulogy provides us with insights into the personality of the subject. It is a warm presentation of praise and acknowledgment of a life well lived.

Eulogies are often associated with funerals and memorial services, but they are occasionally used to honor the living. Information may be obtained by interviewing friends or family members. Local newspapers have files with information that may be easily acquired.

Very personal information about the person or the family that might cause embarrassment should be avoided. The object is to praise positive traits or to remember special memories you or others hold of the person. It is not a time to exaggerate or tell dramatic stories that are not necessarily true. Eulogies provide us with insight into the choices the person made and the things they really wanted from life.

Use the included eulogy form (page 32) to interview friends and family members. For this assignment, it will be helpful if you select a well-known individual. The research for the project can be completed in the library or on the Internet. You may choose to feature individuals you have read about. This would make an excellent choice, since you may already have personal stories or anecdotes to share.

It is interesting to present a background about the person's birth and parents. Including a few stories that happened during the subject's childhood may lend a quality of naturalness and confirm to the listener that the subject is someone with whom we can identify. Also, share obstacles that the person overcame to achieve greatness; these are inspiring and create a feeling of empathy, or connection. The delivery style of the eulogy should be that of a narrative, or very similar to storytelling. Develop a good narrative style that creates an attitude of expectancy on the part of the listener.

We are all acquainted with the public person, but the eulogy serves to grant us glimpses into the private life and personality of the subject.

Example: "Mark Twain fell in love with the river at an early age, and continued to love it until his death. It made him what he was. Perhaps the river appeared to him to be going somewhere he longed to go. The search for adventure would one day lead him to ride the river to a new destiny."

Eulogies *(cont.)*

Subject Form

Complete the following form and deliver your eulogy to the class, using the information on this page as your notes. Select a well-known historical figure or someone you knew personally. Limit your selections to deceased individuals.

Speaker: _____   Subject: _____

Birthplace: _____

Childhood home: _____

Early anecdotes and incidents: _____

_____

_____

Career choice: _____

Family life and family members: _____

_____

Stories involving family: _____

Adult home: _____

Career changes: _____

_____

Most memorable trait: _____

Most memorable quotation or story: _____

_____

Accomplishments: _____

_____

Events that helped shape destiny: _____

_____

_____

_____

Eulogies *(cont.)*

Critique Sheet

Circle one:

      1—Superior   2—Excellent   3—Good   4—Fair

Was delivery expressive and relaxed?

      1   2   3   4

Were the qualities of the individual expressed?

      1   2   3   4

Was the message conveyed in an organized way?

      1   2   3   4

Comments: _____

_____

_____

_____

_____

_____

Questioning Strategies

The ability to question for understanding and to gain knowledge provides us with the power to control destiny and circumstance. Some job interviews are even determined by the applicant's ability to ask, as well as respond to, questions.

Basic questioning skills involve "who," "what," "when," "where," "why," and "how" questions. The higher levels of questioning strategies utilize comprehension of details, analysis, and application. Some well-known interviewers gain notoriety and difficult-to-obtain interviews due to the thoughtfulness and content of the questions they ask. This ability is developed through much practice.

The activities on pages 35–39 will provide you with the opportunity to develop these skills.

Who Am I?

Two students come to the front of the classroom and place desks so that they face each other. One student draws the name of a well-known person or fictional character. He or she is then questioned by the other student until the identity of the person is determined. The questions must require only a "yes" or "no" answer. Other students are not allowed to question but may guess the identity of the character. If the questioner correctly guesses the identity, he or she remains champion. If a class member guesses first, he or she replaces the questioner for the next round. Members of the class should take turns being the one questioned. See the following page for sample questions an interviewer might consider asking.

Questioning Strategies *(cont.)*

Who Am I? *(cont.)*

Sample Questions

Answer with a simple **Yes** or **No**. Do not volunteer additional information.

1. Is the person male/female?	**Yes**	**No**
2. Is he/she fictional?	**Yes**	**No**
3. Is he/she living?	**Yes**	**No**
4. Is he/she a historical character?	**Yes**	**No**
5. Is he/she infamous?	**Yes**	**No**
6. Is he/she an entertainer?	**Yes**	**No**
7. Is he/she a singer?	**Yes**	**No**
8. Does he/she make movies?	**Yes**	**No**
9. Is he/she a cartoon character?	**Yes**	**No**
10. Is he/she a politician?	**Yes**	**No**
11. Has he/she been president?	**Yes**	**No**
12. Is he/she an inventor?	**Yes**	**No**
13. Does he/she have a talk show?	**Yes**	**No**
14. Is he/she a musician?	**Yes**	**No**
15. Is he/she in his/her 30s? 40s? etc.	**Yes**	**No**
16. Was he/she a famous child?	**Yes**	**No**
17. Is he/she associated with a specific product?	**Yes**	**No**
18. Is he/she a sports figure?	**Yes**	**No**
19. Is he/she a news reporter?	**Yes**	**No**
20. Is he/she a writer?	**Yes**	**No**

Questioning Strategies *(cont.)*

What's the Question?

This activity may be completed ahead of time or used as a class participation activity. This worksheet already has answers; it's the job of the students to determine an appropriate question for each answer.

1. _____
   _____

   Answer: cotton candy

2. _____
   _____

   Answer: Martin Luther King, Jr.

3. _____
   _____

   Answer: Goldilocks

4. _____
   _____

   Answer: a touchdown

5. _____
   _____

   Answer: watermelon

6. _____
   _____

   Answer: a hot dog

7. _____
   _____

   Answer: The Big Bad Wolf

8. _____
   _____

   Answer: Peter Pan

Questioning Strategies *(cont.)*

Right Behind You

A group leader or the teacher selects a subject for each individual to discuss. They write the topic on a small card and tape it to each participant's back. Members of the group circulate and ask questions about each person's subject. The winner of the activity guesses his or her subject first. Continue until all subjects are determined. Questions should be general and not obvious; the participants must put together clues. Questions are answered in conversational manner and not with a simple "yes" or "no." Other conversation is encouraged. This activity is also a great ice breaker for a party and helps everyone—even strangers—get acquainted.

Suggestions for Topics

- school subjects
- movies
- TV sitcoms
- time travel
- fast food
- music styles
- dances
- freedoms
- dolls
- singers
- athletes
- dinosaurs
- hobbies
- scary movies
- talk shows
- movie stars

- cartoon characters
- animal stars
- fairy tales
- the Olympics
- vacation spots
- clothing styles
- pets
- cars
- politics
- cities
- careers
- toys
- books
- computers
- animals
- the Internet

Questioning Strategies *(cont.)*

Types of Questions

There are four types of questions. Use the following definitions to answer the questions on the worksheet on page 39.

☞ Direct Questions

There are questions that may be answered in a short answer.

Example: Did you take out the trash?

☞ Open Questions

The respondent may amplify, elaborate, or explain his responses.

Example: Why did you decide to take this class?

☞ Probe Questions

These are similar to open questions, since they also require a longer answer. This question type delves below the surface and asks why a particular decision was made or action was taken.

Example: Why did you return to the scene of the crime?

☞ Leading (or Loaded) Questions

These are usually in courtroom dramas or in disciplinary actions. The respondent is given a series of questions which lead to a breakdown, admission of guilt, or dramatic mistake. Usually the question may only be answered by admitting guilt for a negative behavior. If you answer "yes," that implies that you were guilty at one time. If you answer "no," that implies you are continuing the negative behavior.

Example: Have you stopped speeding on the way to work?

Questioning Strategies *(cont.)*

Types of Questions Worksheet

The following are examples of either direct, open, probe, or leading (loaded) questions. Identify the type of question by writing in the space provided before each question. Use the information provided on page 38 to determine the type of question.

_____ 1. Could you describe your morning classes?

_____ 2. What do you feel this character's motivation was for him to return to the scene of the crime?

_____ 3. Did you have breakfast yet?

_____ 4. Have you stopped running red lights?

_____ 5. Could you describe your new car?

_____ 6. What is causing the high school dropout problem?

_____ 7. Is someone at the door?

_____ 8. Could you describe the person at the door?

_____ 9. Why did he stop and talk to her at that hour of the day?

_____ 10. Did you stop skipping that class?

_____ 11. Did you sharpen your pencil?

_____ 12. Why did you choose that school?

_____ 13. Why did he vote for that candidate?

_____ 14. Are you still skimming the funds?

Teacher Instructions: Fold this section under before copying this page for students.

Answer Key: 1. open 2. probe 3. direct 4. leading 5. open 6. probe 7. direct 8. open 9. probe 10. leading 11. direct 12. open 13. probe 14. leading

The Interview Process

The interview is perhaps the most life-changing type of oral communication we will explore. It is the interview that provides us with jobs, child care, etc.—even a visit to the doctor or a first date may be categorized as a type of interview.

The interview may be defined as a formal exchange of questions and ideas. The information that results from the interview process will often be used to determine a course of action.

The job interview is the most basic interview style we will explore. It is the chance for us to sell our most important commodity: ourselves. The following are some key points to remember when preparing for a interview:

○ It is important to relax, but go prepared with questions you would like to ask.

○ The interviewer should also be prepared with questions, since this decision could be very eventful, and this short interaction may be the beginning of a lifetime working relationship.

○ One key point to remember is to remain positive about yourself and your ability to do the job— but don't work overly hard to impress. Remember, when you try to impress someone, that's the impression you make.

○ Be business-like but warm and friendly. Smile, but don't be overly chatty or say too much about yourself.

○ It is good to come prepared with a resume. A resume is simply a review of your experience, preparation, job skills, and life skills.

○ A first impression is often a lasting impression. Take care with appearance. Business attire is always appropriate for an interview. Clothing should fit well and be comfortable. Avoid appearing overdressed with clothing more appropriate for evening wear. Avoid heavy makeup and perfume. Dress as if you are going to work that day. Nails should be clean and neat. Don't wear either flimsy or heavy footwear for the interview. Quiet colors are also a good choice.

○ Never chew gum or snack during an interview, even if food is offered. It is difficult to express yourself with food in your mouth.

○ Business grammar is best. Don't attempt to establish rapport by using slang or phrases like "yeah," "whatever," "you know," "you see," "and everything," "and stuff," etc. If you have developed a habit of overusing a phrase, be cognizant of it and attempt to stop. It is an irritation to the listener and a barrier to good communication.

○ Ask questions about job expectations, but never ask the interviewer questions about his personal life. You are establishing a business relationship.

○ It is appropriate to inquire about work hours, payment plans, insurance, and benefits if the information is not offered. Just remember to maintain a business-like manner.

The Interview Process *(cont.)*

The Resumé

When a person goes on a job interview, the most important document for him or her to have is usually a resumé. A resumé contains only your most vital job skills and experience. A prospective employer will often base his or her first impression of you on the information contained on your resumé; and while you may not be hired strictly on the strength of your resumé, a poorly written or insufficient resumé may stop you from being granted an interview in the first place. What job skills do you possess? Where have you been employed? For how long were you employed there, and what was your salary? Where did you receive your education? What is your objective or reason for applying for this position? These are all questions that your resumé should efficiently answer.

Letter of Recommendation

It is a good idea to bring letters of reference or recommendations from people you have worked with. These may be from past employers, but if you are just beginning your career, it is a good idea to bring letters from responsible friends, a teacher, or even a neighbor you have helped.

If you have had a favorable experience from a person in authority, it is good to request a letter of recommendation. Most people in these positions expect these requests and often have their own form in their files to complete. (However, a form is included on page 43 to offer so that the recommendation follows a structure.)

When you request and receive the letter or form, keep one copy on file so other copies may be made. Do not keep returning to the same person and request that they complete another form because you lost the previous one.

On the copy you submit to an interested employer, add the name, current address, and phone number of the person so that he or she may be contacted and questioned.

Do not list a recommendation you feel may not be positive. Personality conflicts occur, and these would not be the best recommendations for employment.

Assignment 1: Complete the resumé form on page 42. Save a copy for you files.

Assignment 2: Request a letter of recommendation from someone you have worked for or with. This may be a scout leader, parent of a child for whom you've provided care, neighbor, teacher, or religious leader. (It is generally not a good rule of thumb to use family members for this.) Ask the person to complete this form for you and begin your file of recommendation.

Assignment 3: Select a partner from the class. Prepare to interview with them for a hypothetical position. You and your partner will predetermine what job you are interviewing for. For the class activity, go to the front of the room. Place a desk between the two of you. The interviewer will ask the questions and complete the interview profile sheet. The person being interviewed will also be allowed to question. At the completion, switch roles and have the other person interview for the position.

The Interview Process *(cont.)*

Resumé

Name:_____

Type of position desired:_____

Educational experience:_____

_____

Special interests, activities, and awards:_____

_____

Community activities and involvement: _____

_____

Past job & work-related experience:_____

_____

Special preparation for this job: _____

_____

Hobbies: _____

_____

Family: _____

_____

Statement of purpose (Why do you desire this position?):

_____

_____

_____

_____

The Interview Process *(cont.)*

Letter of Recommendation

1. Name of applicant _____

2. Name of person completing this form _____

_____

3. How long have you known the applicant? _____

4. In what capacity have you known the applicant? (List work or service relationships.)

_____

_____

_____

5. Has this person proved to be dependable? Comments _____

_____

_____

6. Would you recommend this person for this position? Comments_____

_____

_____

7. Evaluate the strengths of this applicant. _____

_____

_____

8. Relate any personal stories or experiences that would aid in making this decision.

_____

_____

_____

The Interview Process *(cont.)*

Interview Questions

1. What is your reason for applying for this position? _____
_____

2. What do you think this position involves? _____
_____

3. How did you learn of the opening? _____
_____

4. Do you know anyone employed by the company?_____
_____

5. What skills could you bring to this position? _____
_____

6. Have you held a position like this in the past?_____
_____

7. What special training have you received to help you in this position?_____
_____

8. What is your educational background? _____
_____

9. What activities do you enjoy?_____
_____

10. Do you live in this area?_____
_____

11. Would a move be difficult? _____
_____

12. What hours would you be available to work?_____
_____

The Interview Process *(cont.)*

Interview Questions *(cont.)*

13. What are your strengths? _____

_____

14. What are your weaknesses? _____

_____

15. What personal goals would you like to achieve in ten years? _____

_____

16. Do you have any special technology skills? _____

_____

17. Would you be willing to accept a lesser position in this company? _____

_____

18. Is there a position that you would not accept with this company? _____

_____

19. How soon would you be available? _____

_____

20. Are you currently employed, and could you be released from your position?

_____

_____

21. Would your spouse be willing to relocate? _____

_____

22. Describe your ideal job: _____

_____

Comments: _____

_____

_____

The Interview Process *(cont.)*

Career Information Interview

Select someone who has a career that interests you and interview him or her. The interview may be conducted by phone, but try to select a time when the person is not on the job, and away from work demands. Share your interview results with the class.

1. Career choice: _____

2. What factors led to this career? _____

   _____

3. What educational experience is required? _____

   _____

4. What other pre-job training was required? _____

   _____

5. What are the most emotionally fulfilling factors of the job? _____

   _____

6. What are the most difficult issues to deal with on the job? _____

   _____

7. Who provides the most help and support for you in the work area? _____

   _____

8. Would you select this career again? _____

9. What is your biggest success or accomplishment in this career? _____

   _____

   _____

   _____

10. Would you advise anyone else to select it? _____

    _____

Persuasive Speech

As citizens of a free society, we have the right to our opinion. We also have the right to try to convince others to believe as we do. The following activities provide the formats we use today for changing public opinion and enlisting the aid of others to support our causes.

Propaganda is a tool of persuasion. This simply means one side of an issue is presented without representation from the other side. The term *propaganda* has developed negative connotations because the information referred to as propaganda is often biased or inaccurate. If a truth is overly emphasized and exaggerated, it can become a fallacy (mistaken belief).

You will be asked to express your opinion, campaign for votes, answer questions, and prepare a commercial. You will resolve situations through problem-solving activities, group discussion, brainstorming, role playing, labor negotiation, conflict resolution, debate, and courtroom debate.

Steps to Effective Persuasion

The following are tools that aid us in persuasion:

- Believe in what you are saying.

- Organize ahead.

- Remain cool and calm.

- Be pleasant.

- Ask for a decision at the conclusion.

- Express the consequences of not adopting this plan or action.

Share Your Opinion

This is your opportunity to express your opinion. Complete the following form and share your answers with the class. Remember, everyone is entitled to his or her own opinion!

1. _____ is the best president who ever served this country.

2. _____ is the best presidential wife.

3. _____ was the greatest American.

4. _____ is the best movie.

5. _____ is the best book.

6. _____ is the greatest writer.

7. _____ is our best sport.

8. _____ is the best university.

9. _____ is the most memorable event in U.S. history.

10. _____ is the most memorable event in world history.

11. _____ is our best actor.

12. _____ is the best ice cream.

13. _____ is the best snack food.

14. _____ is the best TV show.

One-Point Persuasive Speech

Presentation Time: 1 to 3 minutes

This is the speech that convinces the listeners to change or take action. Motivational speaking falls into this category. This is a speech you plan ahead, and a note card may be used. The speech should not be read and also should not appear memorized. Remember, limit the speech to one point or change you wish to see. It is a good idea to avoid very controversial issues for classroom use. In a free society, we are all entitled to our opinion, but it is sometimes difficult for the listener to listen objectively to a point of view he or she strongly opposes. Always remember to keep issues light, or you may become the one that has problems maintaining your composure.

Avoid a memorized-sounding delivery style. This style often runs by the listener like a freight train and leaves him or her dazed in the process. When a speaker is really communicating ideas with the listener, it creates the impression that he or she is thinking of the ideas, much as we think before we speak in general conversation. If the delivery is rapid and delivered from memory and without much thought, it is usually very difficult for the listener to process the ideas. The listener's thought processes are usually a little behind the speaker. This is a natural delay we all experience as we mentally process ideas and concepts. It is much like dancing and following a partner. The leader must be sure the partner is following. An overly memorized-sounding delivery might be likened to a song: while it might be entertaining, and even rhythmic, we still might have to listen to it several times before we fully comprehend it. The key difference, however, is that a speech will be heard only once, and so its message must be understood on the first listen.

Below are some suggested topics to choose from. Select one (or choose your own) and develop your persuasive speech around it. Remember to utilize the tools (listed on page 47) that a speaker can use to make his or her speech more persuasive.

Topics

- Cats/dogs make the best pets.
- Join my club or organization.
- Change your harmful habit.
- Outlaw gasoline engines.
- Vote for this person.
- Support my charity.
- Root for this player.
- Listen to this band.
- Drink more water.
- Exercise.

One-Point Persuasive Speech *(cont.)*

Critique Sheet

Speaker: _____

Evaluator: _____

Circle an evaluation mark in each category and add constructive comments in the provided space.

1—Superior   2—Excellent   3—Good   4—Fair

Delivery Technique:

Facial Expression (relaxed, animated, and responsive):   1   2   3   4

Vocal Expression (variance, rate, pitch, volume, intensity, and inflection):   1   2   3   4

Diction, Grammar, and Word Usage (No "you know's," "um's," or "ah's"):   1   2   3   4

Eye Contact (looks at audience, not overly dependent on notes):   1   2   3   4

Bodily Action and Gestures (relaxed, comfortable stance, no distracting movements, notes handled well):   1   2   3   4

Comments: _____

Organization and Content:

Introduction (attention step):   1   2   3   4

Body (followed organized outline and developed points):   1   2   3   4

Conclusion (summary and closing comments):   1   2   3   4

Comments: _____

Campaign Speech

This is the promotion where the product is you. It allows for questions and answers. A press conference follows this format. It has the following characteristics:

☞ A campaign speech organizes a need for change and details the plan that the candidate, if elected, will rely on to correct existing problems. This is called a platform. The individual steps are called planks.

☞ This type of persuasive speech presents a need for change or endorsement of an idea, product, or individual. After the speech, questions are entertained from "the floor" (those listening to the speech). This type of speech is usually associated with political discussions or the town meeting format.

Presentation Time: 5 minutes

Assignment: Select an office you desire or a change you would like to make. Let these guidelines serve as your guide:

1. Clearly state the office or change you seek.

2. State your qualifications or the need for change.

3. State your plan of service or the advantages to the change.

4. Present conclusions and allow time for questions.

Campaign Speech *(cont.)*

Critique Sheet

Speaker: _____

Evaluator: _____

Circle an evaluation mark in each category and add constructive comments in the provided space.

1—Superior   2—Excellent   3—Good   4—Fair

Delivery Technique:

Facial Expression (relaxed, animated, and responsive):	1	2	3	4
Vocal Expression (variance, rate, pitch, volume, intensity, and inflection):	1	2	3	4
Diction, Grammar, and Word Usage (No "you know's," "um's," or "ah's"):	1	2	3	4
Eye Contact (looks at audience, not overly dependent on notes):	1	2	3	4
Bodily Action and Gestures (relaxed, comfortable stance, no distracting movements, notes handled well):	1	2	3	4

Comments: _____

Organization and Content:

Introduction (attention step):	1	2	3	4
Body (followed organized outline and developed points):	1	2	3	4
Conclusion (summary and closing comments):	1	2	3	4

Comments: _____

Commercials

We are consumers by nature; and recorded advertisements for products—or commercials, as we call them—have become woven into the tapestry of our lives. They are a commonality we share in this culture; they often reflect our tastes in music, humor, and even our core values. A brief, one-minute promo can make us laugh and/or cry—but most of all, buy! We hear advertisements and commercials so much that they have become almost sentimental to us. We enjoy watching them in groups, and treasure nostalgic commercials. We even present awards for commercials.

This activity provides the chance to create your own masterpiece that will be enjoyed by the group.

Assignment: Create your own one-minute commercial. You may do it live in front of the class, videotape it with a video recorder, and use a VCR to present your commercial. You may also record it on a tape recorder, as if it were a radio spot.

The story organizer on page 54 is included as an aid when using various cues. You may also enlist the aid of others to speak, sing, play, and/or act.

Commercials *(cont.)*

Story Organizer

Topic:_____

Outline	Visual Aids	Audio	Actions

Commercials *(cont.)*

Critique Sheet

Circle one:

1—Superior   2—Excellent   3—Good   4—Fair

Was the commercial believable and persuasive?

      1   2   3   4

Was the business planned, precise, and in order?

      1   2   3   4

Were media effects handled well?

      1   2   3   4

Did the commercial communicate the purpose?

      1   2   3   4

Comments: _____

_____

_____

_____

_____

Problem Solving

The Good Neighbors

Develop a step-by-step written plan to solve the problem.

A lady on your block is recently widowed and on a limited income. Winter is coming and her home needs some repairs for her to stay warm and keep her fuel bills low.

What could be done by you and other kids in the neighborhood to help?

State the Problem	**Make a Plan**

Organize Plan Details	**List Outcomes and Advantages**

Problem Solving *(cont.)*

The Garage Sale

Develop a step-by-step written plan to solve the following problem.

A group of students has experienced success with garage sales. They would like to do this on a regular basis when they are not in school. Help them organize this project.

State the Problem	Make a Plan

Organize Plan Details	List Outcomes and Advantages

Problem Solving *(cont.)*

Save the Park!

Develop a step-by-step written plan to solve the following problem.

A much-used neighborhood park has deteriorated. Children still play there and it appears to be safe, but the equipment is old and in need of repair.

State the Problem	**Make a Plan**
Organize Plan Details	**List Outcomes and Advantages**

Problem Solving *(cont.)*

The Field Trip

Develop a step-by-step written plan to solve the following problem.

Your club would love to attend a vacation spot 350 miles away. You must raise the money and plan the trip.

State the Problem	**Make a Plan**
Organize Plan Details	**List Outcomes and Advantages**

Problem Solving *(cont.)*

Yet Another Dilemma

Select a problem of your own. Develop a step-by-step written plan to solve it.

State the Problem	**Make a Plan**
Organize Plan Details	**List Outcomes and Advantages**

Group Discussion

The following are a few types of discussion:

☞ **The Panel Discussion**

Members of the panel, usually experts on a subject, present information. On the basis of this information, the panel draws a conclusion about a future course of action.

☞ **The Round Table Discussion**

In this type of discussion, everyone has a voice. This is the type of discussion that town meetings are based on; it is also the format we will use for the assignment.

Presentation Time: 7 to 10 minutes

Assignment: Form groups of 4 to 6 members. Each group will need planning time before the discussion to select the topic, a leader, and a recorder. It is the leader's task to organize the discussion, bring out quieter members, and make certain no one dominates the time. It is the goal of the group to reach a conclusion or an agreement. Everyone should be open to compromise and explore every part of the topic.

It is best to avoid very emotional or controversial topics. It is usually best if the discussion group has at least one full class period to plan the discussion. First, have groups decide the qualities of good leaders and good listeners (page 62). Next, have the group use the following suggested discussion topics (or choose ones of their own) along with the chart on page 63 to plan their group presentations.

Suggested Discussion Topics

○ establishment of community action groups for recycling and conservation

○ tax vouchers for private schools

○ government-provided medical care for all people under the age of 18

○ the most important events of the 20th century

○ methods needed to reduce the number of drunk drivers

○ liability of tobacco companies toward the consumers of their products

○ teen curfews

○ methods needed to improve education

○ the most influential individuals of this century

○ methods needed to increase teen community involvement and provide more recreational activities

○ raising or lowering the legal driving age

Group Discussion *(cont.)*

Leaders and Listeners

Have groups meet to complete the following activity, which aims to clarify the expectations for leaders and listeners. Each group should choose a leader, whose job it will be to do the following five duties:

○ State topic and open discussion.

○ Establish norms for the group.

○ Reinforce the norms.

○ Keep the group on task.

○ Review future plan of action.

It is the job of the other members of the group to contribute to the discussion and work with the leader to develop a consensus opinion. Each member must intently listen to the others in his or her group. There are two main types of listeners. They are as follows:

☞ **Active Listener**

Takes notes, nods head, questions for understanding, and restates the information to check for understanding.

☞ **Passive Listener**

Listens quietly, but does not cause distractions or appear to be off task.

Presentation Time: 7 to 10 minutes

Assignment: As a group, discuss and answer the following questions. Cite several examples to support your answers.

○ What traits make a good leader?

○ What traits make a poor leader?

○ What traits make a good listener?

○ What traits or distracting qualities make for a poor listener?

Group Discussion *(cont.)*

Decision Making

1. State and understand the problem.
2. Make a plan.
3. Organize plan details.
4. List outcomes and advantages.

Problem: _____

(Topic of your choice)

Plan	Plan Details	Outcomes

Group Discussion *(cont.)*

Review

1. Topic: _____

_____

2. In favor of change and points expressed: _____

_____

_____

_____

_____

_____

_____

3. In opposition of change and points presented: _____

_____

_____

_____

_____

_____

_____

4. Conclusion of the group: _____

_____

_____

_____

_____

Group Discussion *(cont.)*

Critique Sheet

Circle one:

　　　1—Superior　　　2—Excellent　　　3—Good　　　4—Fair

1. Did participants seem involved in the activity?	1　2　3　4
2. Did each speaker attempt to persuade the decision in his or her favor?	1　2　3　4
3. Were arguments believable?	1　2　3　4
4. Were speakers consistent throughout the activity?	1　2　3　4
5. Was a compromise reached?	1　2　3　4

6. Who made the biggest compromise?_____

7. Who presented the strongest arguments? _____

8. Did you agree with the decision of the group? _____ Explain: _____

　　_____

　　_____

9. Did the participants have equal time? _____

10. Was there a balance of power, without some dominant and some passive members?_____

11. Were the participants listening to each other?_____

12. Was the leadership effective but not controlling?_____

13. If you were a judge in this situation, what would be your decision?_____

　　_____

14. Did all members of the group appear to agree with the final decision?

　　_____

　　_____

Comments: _____

　　_____

Group Discussion *(cont.)*

Brainstorming

Brainstorming is used to enlist everyone's creative responses to a problem. Follow these simple steps:

☞   The whole group participates. A leader and a recorder are selected.

☞   The problem is stated. Then everyone contributes their ideas. At this time, workability is not discussed. The recorder simple writes down the ideas presented.

☞   When enough ideas are presented, the leader has the recorder read each one individually and the group discusses problems or workability arguments.

☞   Workable ideas are listed and the group selects the most favorable plans.

☞   The future plan of action is determined by the group.

☞   No put downs are to be given during either the brainstorming session or when the group is discussing workability and future actions.

The leader will need to regulate the schedule the group follows. The brainstorming session will begin with many ideas. Allow everyone to contribute. As ideas begin to wane, the leader should move the group to the next phase: the workability of all the arguments. The entire session should be recorded by the recorder on the web provided (page 67). The leader will need to keep the discussion moving, regulate the time, and help the group determine a future course of action.

Presentation Time: 3 to 5 minutes

Assignment: Select a topic from the list below or create one of your own. Use the web provided on page 67 to map the problem. After brainstorming and mapping the problem, the leader should present to the class his or her group's solution and thought process in arriving at that solution.

Topics

- fundraising ideas

- encouraging parental involvement in school activities

- planning a youth and recreational center

- establishing a community theater

- increasing student participation in school activities

- raising student achievement test scores

- improving the school lunch program

Group Discussion *(cont.)*

Brainstorming Web

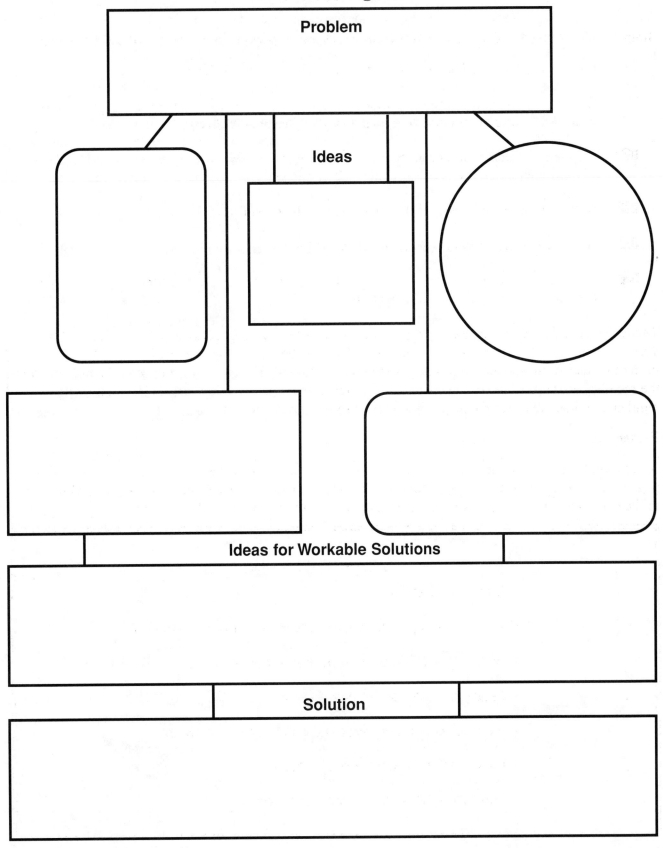

Problem

Ideas

Ideas for Workable Solutions

Solution

Labor Negotiation

Presentation Time: 10 to 15 minutes

Assignment: This is a role play exercise that addresses the everyday type of problems that occur in the work place. It is intended to enrich students' skills in negotiation and the powers involved in both persuasion and compromise. Form groups of six and complete the following steps:

☞ Choose a leader and a recorder.

☞ Base the characters on the detailed descriptions provided on page 69. Apart from the negotiator, all other members are employees of the Easy-Life Food Company. The negotiator has been hired by the company to reach a peaceful compromise in this decision. Each member should assume his or her role and persuade the others in the group that he or she should get the new truck. It should be noted that it has been the past policy of the company to make similar decisions based on seniority.

☞ It is recommended that members of the group be seated in a circle. If a rectangular table is used, the negotiator should be seated at the end or in the middle.

☞ It is important for the class to watch and critique each group. As we observe others using persuasive tactics and attempting compromise, we learn and develop skills in these areas. It is also good to have a class discussion about the role play, if time permits.

☞ Look for personality types like the Charmer, the Whiner, the Martyr, the Pouter, the Salesperson, and even those who misunderstand to gain position. However, it should be understood that this is a role play to gain insight and not a personal critique of those doing the role playing.

☞ Have fun with this!

Labor Negotiation *(cont.)*

Roles

Terry: A negotiator hired by the company. Terry is the leader and wishes only to reach a compromise that assigns the new truck and retires the old one. The other trucks may be reassigned to other group members and even repaired at the company's expense. The leader encourages all persons to be allowed to represent their cases and desires a happy compromise.

Jo: 20 years with the company and has a 1-year-old truck. Jo has an excellent work record and received a new truck—which now has 15,000 miles on it—last year. Jo feels the decision must be based on seniority.

Pat: 15 years with the company and has a 3-year-old truck. Pat has a good work record and high sales. Pat feels that since he/she has more customers than most, it is important to drive fast. Pat has had a few fender benders in the last year, and the truck has not been repaired. The truck is in great shape mechanically, and Pat feels it should be repaired and passed down the line. Pat agrees the decision must be based on seniority, and feels he/she is next in line since Jo got the truck last year.

Lynn: 10 years with the company and has a 4-year-old truck. Lynn's truck still looks like new but has been in the repair shop three times this year. Lynn hates to miss work because of mechanical problems and is a single parent who cannot afford unpaid days off of work. Lynn wants a dependable truck and feels it is deserved because of an excellent driving record. Lynn has the lowest sales, which can be attributed to time off work for mechanical failures and family problems.

Tracy: 3 years with the company and has a 2-year-old truck. Tracy's truck is in good shape, but the food refrigeration unit keeps breaking and the ice cream and frozen foods thaw. Tracy is also the child of the owner of the company and feels entitled to a new truck.

Sydney: 1 year with the company and has a 5-year-old truck. Sydney has an old truck in fair mechanical shape, but the heater doesn't work and Sydney has been ill all winter. Despite colds and a case of the flu, Sydney just keeps on working and is now the top salesperson in the company. Sydney was named the salesperson of the year and is also the district's outstanding new employee. Sydney delivers to nearly twice as many customers as any other salesperson and is often on the road 12 hours a day. Sydney feels the senior members have great trucks already, and trucks should go to the people working to bring in the money to pay for them.

Labor Negotiation *(cont.)*

Critique Sheet

Circle one:

1—Superior   2—Excellent   3—Good   4—Fair

Did members maintain believable characters and arguments?

1   2   3   4

Was the discussion well-balanced with all needs presented?

1   2   3   4

Were members willing to compromise?

1   2   3   4

Did members really listen and relate to each other?

1   2   3   4

Comments: _____

_____

_____

_____

_____

One-on-One Conflict Resolution

The following are examples of the daily conflicts we all encounter. Each conflict is designed for two participants. Resolutions should take place when participants are seated at a table in front of the class.

◆ Conflict 1: Neighbors

The dog next door likes to dig in flower beds. The owner has been warned about the dog's straying ways. Now the dog has dug up a rare flower scheduled for a flower show this week. The police were called and the dog did not have tags and is now in the pound. Who will pay the bail? Will the dog owner compensate the neighbor for the destroyed flower?

◆ Conflict 2: Housemates

One resident works long hours and likes to go to bed early. The other needs to entertain for business, keeps late hours, and has very noisy guests.

◆ Conflict 3: Siblings

One just discovered the other has been using his/her credit card without permission. The other meant to pay it off, but now does not have the money to do so.

◆ Conflict 4: Store Owner/Employee

The employee is a personal friend and an excellent salesperson. Recently, the employee has been coming in late for work. One night the store had to close early because the employee did not show up and there was no one there to work.

◆ Conflict 5: Teacher/Student

An important term paper is due on a set date. The date was given at the beginning of the course. The student is in line for an important scholarship and needs an "A" in the class. He/she was busy and did not turn in the paper until the next day. Other students in the class turned in their papers on time and desire the same scholarship. The paper is "A" quality, but should it receive that grade even though it was a day late—or should it even be accepted at all?

◆ Conflict 6: Parent/Child

A young teenager is invited to a single-gender party at a local motel with an indoor pool and recreational facilities. There will be no adults present, but one of the teenager's 18-year-old siblings will supervise the party.

◆ Conflict 7: Teacher/Parent

A parent is concerned that his/her child is enduring bullies in the teacher's class. The teacher feels the parent's child does a lot to fuel the situation, but he/she has made attempts to correct the bullies. What can be done?

◆ Conflict 8: Friends

These people have been friends for many years. One has a backyard pool and allows the neighbor pool use. Lately, the neighbor has been bringing two noisy friends to swim after the owners have gone to bed. The family is not sleeping well when it is noisy.

◆ Conflict 9: Neighbors

Each rent a different side of a duplex. They agreed to share gardening expenses. They have contracted someone to mow each week, but the bills come to one neighbor. The other neighbor is far behind in payments and now says he/she can mow his/her own lawn. He/she will not pay the amount owed for the last three months but is still not mowing the lawn, so the other neighbor is still paying to have it mowed.

◆ Conflict 10: Your Choice

Choose a conflict of your own. The conflict should be resolved.

One-On-One
Conflict Resolution *(cont.)*

Critique Sheet

Team: _____

Evaluator: _____

Circle one rating in each category and add constructive comments in the space provided.

1—Superior   2—Excellent   3—Good   4—Fair

1. Did both participants seem involved in the activity?   1   2   3   4

2. Did each character attempt to persuade a decision
   in his favor?   1   2   3   4

3. Were arguments believable?   1   2   3   4

4. Were characters consistent throughout the activity?   1   2   3   4

5. Was a compromise reached?   1   2   3   4

6. Who made the biggest compromise?_____

7. Who presented the strongest arguments? _____

8. What arguments would you have emphasized?_____

9. Did you agree with the decision? _____

10. Explain the reasons you agree or disagree with the arguments. _____

    _____

11. If you were a judge in this situation, what would be your decision?_____

    _____

12. Did the participants have equal time and make equal contributions? _____

    _____

13. Was one member more passive or dominant than the other? _____

    _____

14. Were they listening to each other? _____

Comments: _____

Debate

Debate is simply defined as a formal argument in which rules and guidelines are followed and a decision is determined.

Debate allows us to accomplish the following:

- present one issue at a time.
- provide equal opportunity for the presentation of each point-of-view.

The skills we develop as a debater allow us to . . .
- collect, organize, and evaluate ideas
- speak convincingly and with clarity and impact
- see logical connections
- listen to, question, and evaluate evidence

Debate is used in decision making in courtrooms, legislative bodies, and educational systems. In a democracy, the ability and right to question is a highly valued freedom.

Debate centers around a proposition. There are three types of propositions:

☞ Proposition of Fact

This type is used in courtrooms, often to determine guilt or innocence.

☞ Proposition of Value

This type of debate is an analysis of basic belief systems. It is this type of proposition that makes up much of political debate—and is often very controversial.

☞ Proposition of Policy

This is the debate of the present state or status quo and the future action to be taken. This is the style used in competitive debate. Students of this style learn to debate both sides of an issue.

Most competitive debate today falls under two categories:

☞ Lincoln-Douglas Debate

Named for political candidates (Abraham Lincoln and Stephen Douglas), it is a debate between two individuals.

☞ Cross Examination Debate

This involves a two-person team with specific speaking responsibilities. This team challenges other two-person teams and advances in a tournament. They debate both sides of the proposition. Each speaker delivers two timed speeches. Speakers may question or cross examine each other after the first speech or the constructive speech.

There are two sides to every debate.

1. One team desires a change in the present system. They are called the affirmative team.

2. The other team desires to maintain and defend the present system. They are called the negative team.

A Lincoln-Douglas Debate

Select a partner and one of the following topics, and complete the form. Then list the disadvantages in the negative space.

Topics

- ○ Raise the driving age to 17.
- ○ Build a youth activity center.
- ○ Make schooling year-round.
- ○ Divide schools by gender.
- ○ Require students to pass achievement tests prior to grade promotion.
- ○ Increase the use of government money for funding the arts.
- ○ Require scholastic requirements for graduation.
- ○ Make school uniforms mandatory.

Presentation Time: 5 minutes

Assignment: In the "affirmative" space, list the advantages of adopting a new policy on your chosen topic. Then, in the "negative" space, list the disadvantages. When the analysis below is complete, you and your partner will debate the issue.

- The *affirmative* speaker will speak first and list the advantages of the proposition.
- The *negative* speaker speaks last and lists the disadvantages.

Topic: _____

Affirmative	Negative

Critique Sheet and Ballot

Affirmative

Comments: _____

_____

_____

_____

_____

_____

Negative

Comments: _____

_____

_____

_____

_____

In my opinion, the most convincing arguments were presented by the . . .

_____ Affirmative Team   _____ Negative Team

(Check one of the above.)

Persuasive Speech

A Cross Examination Debate

Presentation Time: 25 to 30 minutes (5 minutes for each speaker; 2 minutes for each rebuttal)

Assignment: Select a partner and an opposing team. Each team will debate two rounds. The teams will both prepare an affirmative plan and a negative case. The rounds may be held on the same day or on different days. Each team will debate both the affirmative and the negative sides of the issue. (A list of issues for debate is given on page 77.) This develops skill in looking at both sides of an issue.

○ The affirmative team supports the resolution, or a change in the present system or the status quo.

○ The negative team supports maintaining the present system and feels the change will only bring more problems rather than solving the need presented by the affirmative team.

Each team will prepare a 5-minute speech. A time keeper will be needed and time cards will be used. The speeches will be presented in the following order:

☞ **1st Affirmative Speaker**

This speaker presents the need to change the present system. This is called a need/plan case. This speaker can also present the advantages of the change and this is called the comparative advantage plan. In either speech the needs must be numbered as needs 1, 2, etc. If advantages are used, they also must be numbered. This speaker tells us which type of case he is using. He must urge for a change.

☞ **1st Negative Speaker**

This speaker urges us to maintain the present system called the status quo. This speaker attacks either the needs or advantages presented by the 1st affirmative speaker and requests our vote.

☞ **2nd Affirmative Speaker**

This speaker must present a step by step plan for the change. Be specific: state how the plan will be paid for, how it will be adopted, and how it will work.

☞ **2nd Negative Speaker**

This speaker attacks the workability of the plan and shows us how it will work. The speaker states that the plan is not a significant change and/or not needed. This ends the speeches that construct the plan. They are called constructive speeches. Each speaker now has a brief chance to answer attacks. These speeches are called rebuttals.

☞ **1st Negative Speaker Rebuttal**

This speaker restates the need or advantage attacks.

☞ **1st Affirmative Speaker Rebuttal**

This speaker restates and reviews the needs or advantages.

☞ **2nd Negative Speaker Rebuttal**

This speaker reviews the plan attacks.

☞ **2nd Affirmative Speaker Rebuttal**

This speaker reviews the affirmative plan.

A Cross-Examination Debate *(cont.)*

You may choose one of the following topics to use for your debate, or you may decide on one of your own.

Topics
We should establish a national program for youth volunteers for community service.
Cafeterias in schools should have a student board of control.
The local school board should elect students to serve with adults.
We need a federally set curriculum and national testing system for both public and private schools.
Year-round schools shall be established nationwide.
Youths should be required to volunteer 30 hours of community service yearly.
Curfews should be established in areas with high crime rates.
Establish gender-choice schools.
Local city council will establish a league of youth officers.
Teen councils will be established to aid juvenile offenders.
A national system of health care will be established for children under 18.
A local agency that deals with student behavior problems will be established.
A system of alternative education will be established nationwide.
A local board will be established to deal with youthful violent offenders.
A national TV network, operated by citizens under age 18, will be established.

A Cross-Examination Debate *(cont.)*

Flow Charts

1st Affirmative Speaker (advantages to changing the status quo)	2nd Affirmative Speaker (plan)

1st Negative Speaker (refutation of advantages to changing status quo)	2nd Negative Speaker (refutation of plan and workability arguments)

A Cross-Examination Debate *(cont.)*

Critique Sheet and Ballot

Affirmative

Comments: _____

_____

_____

_____

_____

_____

Negative

Comments: _____

_____

_____

_____

_____

_____

In my opinion, the most convincing arguments were presented by the . . .

_____ Affirmative Team   _____ Negative Team

(Check one of the above.)

In the Courtroom

Cast the following characters and follow the procedure below to create a courtroom debate.

Characters

- judge

- one defendant

- two prosecution lawyers

- two defense lawyers

- three witnesses for the defense

- three witnesses for the prosecution

- jury (The rest of the class. They will vote to determine verdict.)

Procedure

1. The case is introduced by a student's accuser.

2. Witnesses present testimony against the accused. (Each is cross-examined by the defense.)

3. Witnesses present testimony for the defense. (Each is examined by the prosecution.)

4. One prosecutor addresses jury with closing remarks.

5. One defense attorney addresses jury with closing remarks.

6. Jury votes by ballot. They inform the judge of verdict.

7. Judge announces verdict. Judge may also sentence.

Note: The jury may select a foreperson to hand the verdict to the judge. The judge may then hand the verdict back to the foreperson, who will announce the verdict.

In the Courtroom *(cont.)*
Court Case Suggestions

The following suggestions provide a defendant (person charged) and the crimes he/she/it is being charged with.

Defendant: Little Red Hen

Charges: bread manufacturing without a license, tax fraud, and refusal to share with neighbors

Tale: The Hen planted some wheat, harvested it, ground it into flour, and baked bread. Through each step of the process, she requested help from her neighbors. They refused until the bread was baked, and then they wanted to eat.

Defendant: Humpty Dumpty

Charges: malicious intent to deface the king's wall, loitering, and creation of a public nuisance.

Tale: *Humpty Dumpty*
Sat on a wall.
Humpty Dumpty had a great fall.
All the king's horses and all the king's men
couldn't put Humpty together again.

Defendant: Little Red Riding Hood

Charges: refusal to share her goods or goodies with an endangered species; suspicion of gang involvement due to continual wearing and identification of her colors

Tale: She was taking a basket of goodies to grandma's when a wolf lurking asked for a taste of the goodies. She is named because she always wears her red cape with a red hood. Little Red traveled on, but the wolf raced ahead and got rid of grandma. He put on her cap and nightgown, and got into grandma's bed so Little Red would give him the goodies.

Defendant: Chicken Little

Charges: desire to willfully endanger others through misrepresentation and fraud

Tale: felt an acorn hit her head and went to warn her fowl barnyard friends that the sky was falling; they were going to tell the king, but were eaten by the fox.

Defendant: Frog that went courtin'

Charges: riding without permit, appropriate saddle, and gear; ignoring public safety

Tale: Children's song with many verses about a frog that courted his friend. Each verse tells of him riding his horse.

Defendant: Oh-Susanna

Charges: loitering and creating an emotional scene in a public walkway

Tale: A song about a weeping woman, longing for her friend who went to Alabama with a banjo on his knee.

In the Courtroom *(cont.)*

Court Case Suggestions *(cont.)*

Defendant: Kermit the Frog

Charges: fraud and breaking of verbal contractual agreement to marry and financially support Miss Piggy (He publicly proposed but has never honored his commitment.)

Defendant: Spider

Charges: frightened and endangered the life of a Miss Muffet; failure to replace financial loss of curds and whey

Tale: *Little Miss Muffet sat on a tuffet [mushroom]*
eating her curds and whey [cottage cheese].
Along came a spider & sat down beside her,
and frightened Miss Muffet away.

Defendant: Dorothy of Kansas

Charges: theft—one pair of ruby red slippers

Tale: Character from the Wizard of Oz. She got her ruby red slippers from the feet of the wicked witch whom she accidentally killed.

Defendant: Little Bo Peep

Charges: maintaining livestock out of zoning area, animal neglect.

Tale: *[Little Bo Peep] lost her sheep and doesn't know where to find them.*
Leave them alone, and they'll come home,
wagging their tails behind them.

Defendant: Baa Baa Black Sheep

Charges: willful failure to provide contracted goods (wool); deliberate prejudicial treatment of Boy in the Lane

Tale: *Baa Baa Black Sheep*   *One for the Master,*
Have you any wool?   *and one for the Dame,*
Yes Sir, Yes Sir,   *but none for the little boy*
three bags full.   *who cries in the lane.*

Defendant: Rip Van Winkle

Charges: use of harmful intoxicating substance; willful neglect of spouse and children; failure to provide adequate support

Tale: Early American tale of character who went into the Catskills for an afternoon walk. He was coaxed into playing nine pins (bowling) with a group of little men. They offered him enchanted brew, which put him to sleep for 20 years. When he awoke, he went into the town and discovered he had missed the last 20 years.

Defendant: Tooth Fairy

Charges: breaking and entering private residences

Tale: A little mystical fairy who exchanges money for baby teeth that were recently lost and hidden under pillows.

Drama

Drama, or the art of relating stories, is present in every human culture. We are emotional beings, and this is a way we learn to cope with serious situations. Drama has also been used around the evening fire to entertain. In this section, you will have the opportunity to explore these expressive methods of telling stories. These include pantomime, oral interpretation of both prose and poetry, storytelling, creative dramatics with improvisation, readers' theater, and melodrama. These tools of expression enlighten our understanding of ourselves, organize our values, and help us to communicate with others.

There are simple differences in the art forms:

☞ Pantomime

Actions without speech or props

☞ Oral Interpretation

Reading either prose or poetry from a script and emoting with voice, facial expression, and eye contact

☞ Storytelling

Relating stories without a script from memory or creating as told

☞ Creative Dramatics and Improvisation

Performing without a written script

☞ Readers' Theater

Cast reads from a script and uses oral interpretation, rather than acting, for dramatic effect

☞ Melodrama

Old fashioned, exaggerated form of play that uses key characters of a hero, heroine, and villain; end result is always that goodness and virtue triumph over all.

Pantomime

Presentation Time: 1 to 2 minutes

A pantomime is a performance of a simple, everyday activity. It is a physical activity that is performed with much attention to detail. No props are used. The performer cannot speak or make any noises. It is totally silent. This has become a popular form of street entertainment and is often done in a black leotard with white clown makeup. The performers are often referred to as mimes.

Select one of the following activities, and use the art of pantomime to perform it for the class. If preferred, cut along the dotted lines, fold the resulting strips, place them in a hat, and randomly select an activity to pantomime.

Pantomime Suggestions
sweeping & locking up
applying makeup before an imaginary mirror
washing a window
walking on a high ledge or tightrope
putting a pet into a pet carrier
building a snowman
eating spaghetti
eating something that is too hot
trying on clothes
being a baseball player
riding in a bus with a reckless driver
eating a snow cone
chopping or peeling onions
drinking a very sour drink
tasting a friend's recipe that tastes very bad
reading a newspaper
following a recipe
being a waiter
walking through snow and throwing snowballs
wrapping a package
chewing gum and blowing bubbles
playing hopscotch
being a basketball player
listening to frightful noises in the house at night
decorating a cake

Pantomine *(cont.)*

Critique Sheet

Circle one:

1—Superior   2—Excellent   3—Good   4—Fair

Did members maintain believable characters and situations?

1   2   3   4

Was the performer believable?

1   2   3   4

Were movements planned, precise, and in order?

1   2   3   4

Was facial expression animated?

1   2   3   4

Comments: _____

_____

_____

_____

_____

_____

Non-Verbal Communication

Zapped

This is a game for any age group. The point of the game is to communicate without speaking.

Teacher Instructions: Prepare squares of folded paper, one for each participant. Place a dot on one of the squares; leave the other squares blank. Cut out the squares and then fold each of them so that no one can see the dot. Place the squares in a container and have each participant draw one. The person who draws the dot is the zapper. He or she should tell no one.

Rules of the Game

1. Each player—including the zapper—receives a form (page 87). The object is to, without speaking, get a different person to sign each line of the form. (Players may allow someone to sign more than one line if everyone else has signed and there are still blank lines left.)

2. The zapper must attempt to zap people by winking at an individual without drawing the attention of the other players. If he winks at everyone before he is discovered, he wins the game.

3. When someone is winked at, they are out of the game. They may no longer try to complete their form. Also, they may not reveal the identity of the zapper to those still in the game.

4. The game may also be won by contestants who complete the form before everyone is zapped. Just announce you are the winner when the form is completed. Do not speak until that point!

5. Another way to win the game is to announce correctly who the zapper is. This cannot be done when he has zapped you. You must observe him zapping someone else. If you proclaim someone the zapper and are incorrect, you are out of the game.

6. Anyone who speaks for any reason other than those previously mentioned is disqualified from the game.

Non-Verbal Communication *(cont.)*

Zapped Form

1. I played in a piano recital. _____

2. My favorite color is red. _____

3. This is my natural hair color. _____

4. I have a cat. _____

5. My car is a Chevy. _____

6. My favorite day is Saturday. _____

7. I sleep upstairs. _____

8. I like strawberries. _____

9. My favorite holiday is Thanksgiving. _____

10. I like olives. _____

11. I play a musical instrument. _____

12. I love dogs. _____

13. I like cauliflower. _____

14. I like the Three Stooges. _____

15. I like to tell jokes. _____

16. I watch the soaps. _____

17. I like football. _____

18. I've been in a play. _____

19. I like to read. _____

20. I like to talk. _____

Oral Interpretation of Poetry

Presentation Time: 5 to 7 minutes

Each student may select a poem or a song and read it for the class. If short selections are chosen, several may be used. The poem may be from a children's book, a serious or humorous poem, or a song. Song choices might be from old rock 'n' roll, country, or even rap. It is very humorous to hear "Your Cheatin' Heart," "(You Ain't Nothin' but a) Hound Dog," or "Why Do Fools Fall in Love?" interpreted as serious poetry. Have fun with this; or, be very dramatic and emote!

It is important to have the script typed or printed large enough so that it may be read without difficulty. It is fine to use a book or even music, but it will be easier to handle if single sheets are put in folders or page savers.

Remember to look up and establish good eye contact with the listeners. Reveal to the listener the emotion you are expressing through your voice and facial expressions.

Should you select to interpret something humorous, remember that it is very difficult to remain poised and in control when things are funny! Remain very calm and interpret it as if you were reading a serious selection. The reader should not be laughing along with the audience.

It is permissible to sing a line or two when interpreting, but most lines should be spoken. It is great to emphasize rhythm for effect. Use your own creativity! The selection always must be read from a script. If it is not, it is not interpretation!

Oral Interpretation of Poetry *(cont.)*

Critique Sheet

Circle one:

      1—Superior   2—Excellent   3—Good   4—Fair

Choice of selection

      1   2   3   4

Did the reader have a relaxed stance and body mannerisms?

      1   2   3   4

Was the selection easily heard?

      1   2   3   4

Did the reader establish communication through facial and vocal expression?

      1   2   3   4

Comments: _____

_____

_____

_____

Drama

Oral Interpretation of Prose

Presentation Time: 7 to 10 minutes

This is often our earliest form of entertainment in our lives. Who cannot remember begging for another bedtime story? Most of us, no doubt, can remember our favorites. It was especially entertaining when the reader used different voices: the Big Bad Wolf was no longer so frightening when he sounded very silly. That is exactly what prose interpretation is. The reader simply reads a story aloud from a printed script. He may use voice, facial expressions, and eye contact to establish different moods and expressions. This is what makes it interpretation!

Assignment: Select a short story to read aloud to the class. Adhere to the following guidelines:

1. Make sure the script is easy to hold and read. Practice ahead so that you become familiar with the script.

2. The story should not be more than 10 minutes long. If it is a little long, cut out the parts that are not essential to the storyline.

3. Provide a brief introduction that includes the title and author. Provide some background about the story or relate why it appeals to you.

4. Establish a pace that is easily followed, and use vocal inflection to create variety.

5. Eye contact and good facial expressions are the keys to good interpretation.

6. Eliminate any unnecessary movement. The interpreter stands in only one spot and holds a script. He or she uses only voice, face, and eyes to show emotion. Any extra movement puts it into the category of mono-acting rather than interpretation.

Oral Interpretation
of Prose *(cont.)*

Critique Sheet

Circle one:

      1—Superior   2—Excellent   3—Good   4—Fair

Choice of selection

    1   2   3   4

Did the reader have a relaxed stance and body mannerisms?

    1   2   3   4

Was the selection easily heard?

    1   2   3   4

Did the reader establish communication through facial and vocal expression?

    1   2   3   4

Comments: _____

_____

_____

_____

_____

Storytelling

The art of storytelling has been around almost as long as humans have. Stories have been passed down as family treasures to be taken out, enjoyed, wrapped in memories, and carefully tucked away to be cherished by yet another generation. The stories of how our families came to settle where they did; how they survived hard times; how our parents, grandparents, and aunts and uncles met and married have become the keynote speeches of the family dinners.

The ability to relate a story well is a skill that will enrich everyone's lives and create emotional ties between new generations of our families and friends. These are the stories most requested by separated or adopted children. The stories provide us with a sense of belonging and a secure place in the world.

Stories are priceless gifts that should not be lost with the passing of our family members but should be filed away to be discovered and treasured by future generations. The struggles our families faced to settle a new world and our victories over those struggles provide our strength to overcome future struggles that we—or our children—might face.

We are all survivors of the perils of the ages and have in our families stories of the Civil War, westward expansion, persecution, and the fabric that makes up the history of mankind. It is this treasure that this unit addresses. Develop and preserve these stories and the ability to relate them.

The activities that follow (pages 93–100) provide the format and opportunity to develop these storytelling skills. The stories may be organized by use of an organizer called the storyboard. The stories need not be written out but rather organized in topical format, or outline, and related to the group.

Various types of stories are explored. You will have the opportunity to develop skills using different story formats.

Storytelling: Share The Ending

The following story needs an ending. Use the storyboard organizer on page 94 to add to or change the story. Have someone in the class read the beginning of the story, and then class members take turns sharing the ending they have created from the storyboard. Do not write the story out and read it; just organize your special ending, and stand and tell it to the class.

The Quail and the Bell

Long ago, in a small village by the sea, there lived a beautiful maiden and her grandmother. They lived in a poor, small cottage and had few worldly possessions, but they were healthy, happy, and had many friends. The grandmother worried about the things that could happen to them with little money, but she could only hope for a better provision someday.

One day, the beautiful maiden was walking along the road in front of their home. She saw a quail caught in a homemade snare. The look in the quail's eyes caused her to feel sympathy for the trapped creature. She walked over to the snare and quickly released the bird. When the quail was released, it did not fly away but, much to her surprise, spoke to her! "Because your heart is filled with mercy for the unfortunate, I will reward you with a special bell. It is the ring of this bell that will grant you one wish."

The maiden thanked the quail and quickly returned home with the bell. Soon her grandmother's health failed, and to make matters worse, they received notice from the owner of their cottage to vacate the premises. The grandmother urged the maiden to move to a larger village where she would find work. The grandmother was no longer able to make the long journey. The maiden knew that her grandmother would not fare well if left alone.

What should the maiden do?

Storytelling: Share the Ending (cont.)

Storyboard Organizer

Topic:_____

Characters	Action	Outcomes

Storytelling: To Be Continued . . .

This storytelling style is a great activity for a party, as it usually ends up being very humorous. It is often called a round robin story. One person begins the story, and each person adds more plot. It is usually a good signal between storytellers to use a bridge such as "and then. . . ."

Assignment: Read the beginning of the story and pre-plan your plot and characters using the story organizer in this unit. Do not write out the story, but organize it ahead so that you will be ready. This story is constructed in such a way that individual stories can be told and connected to the main story.

Mansion Memories

Once upon a time in a village in Anywhere, U.S.A., a group of teenagers wanted to contribute something to the community. Much concern was expressed over a deteriorating old house in the heart of the community. The house had been historically significant to the town for the last century. Now it was vacant and an eyesore.

Everyone hated to see such a lovely old home with such a rich history destroyed! The group set about to discover the true history of the house and what could be done to aid in its preservation. Many rumors circulated about the events that had happened at the house. The house had stood in that spot for over a century. Many families had come and gone and left their mark on the house and the town. It was up to the group of teenagers to find out the history. The group decided to interview local citizens to determine the truth behind the rumors. It was even rumored that some tenants had fled from fright.

The group soon learned from the interviews that many colorful characters and situations lived in the mansion. . . .

Storytelling:
To Be Continued . . . *(cont.)*

Storyboard Organizer

Topic:_____

Characters	Action	Outcomes

Storytelling: Retelling the Tale

This unit provides the storyteller with a chance to retell an old or well-known story or fairytale. This may also be a book or movie. The story should provide a new slant or take a new twist at the end. This may be humorous, serious, or dramatic.

Suggestions:

◆ Change character types.

The wolf in *Little Red Riding Hood* could become the protagonist (good guy), while Little Red Riding Hood becomes the antagonist (bad guy).

◆ Create a modern version of a well-known story.

Example: Snow White and the Homeboys of the Hood

◆ Mix bits of stories and characters into a new version.

Example: The Big Bad Wolf tells how he has been viciously slandered when all he ever wanted was a good meal!

◆ Develop a familiar story into a poem or a rap.

◆ Select a well-known song and make it into a story.

Example: The Old Gray Mare sues for age discrimination and is put out to pasture!

◆ Select a well-known historical story or myth and retell it.

Example: Washington and the cherry tree encounter the Cherry Pickers' Union.

◆ Select a story or nursery rhyme and enlighten us on what has happened to update the original.

Example: Mr. H. Dumpty sues the King's Men for irreparable damage and negligence.

Storytelling: Retelling the Tale *(cont.)*

Storyboard Organizer

Topic: _____

Characters	Action	Outcomes

Storytelling: Chill Out

No storytelling unit would be complete without the tale of terror. The "gotcha'" stories are in this category also. A gotcha' story is one that sounds frightening and is filled with suspense. At the end the storyteller yells out and grabs someone close saying "Gotcha'!" These stories are often related in the dark, at camp outs, and at slumber parties. No doubt you have already heard many.

This is a story type that allows the storyteller to set the mood. The speaker may build suspense by using facial expressions or vocal inflections. A good storyteller can scare the daylights out of his or her listeners! The success of recent horror movies shows us that many of us love to be scared. Perhaps it is a way of confronting our fears and making us see how silly they really are. There are classic tales of terror that have been told for generations.

Assignment: Prepare and tell a tale of terror you have heard, or create an original. Use the storyboard organizer on page 100 to prepare your story and share it with the class. The following is a list of classic tales of terror that circulate today. These might help you select your own tale of terror.

○ The Man with the Hook Arm

○ The Hitchhiker

○ A babysitter gets a call from a murderer who claims he is calling from inside the house.

○ A girl is followed home by a man who keeps turning on his bright lights, only to discover he is trying to protect her from the person hiding in her back seat.

○ The girl at the slumber party who goes to the grave to plunge in a letter opener to prove to others she is not afraid. She unknowingly plunges it into the hem of her nightgown. It pins her to the grave; and thinking she is being grabbed by the living dead, she dies of fright.

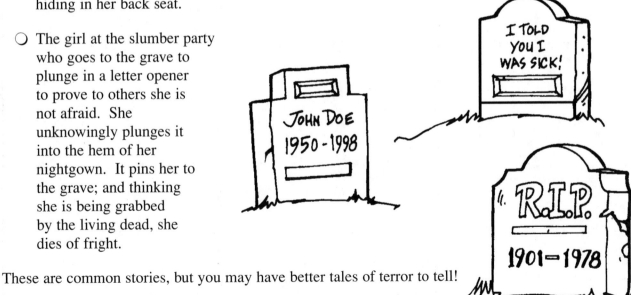

These are common stories, but you may have better tales of terror to tell!

Storytelling: Chill Out *(cont.)*

Storyboard Organizer

Topic: _____

Characters	Action	Outcomes

Storytelling: Urban Legends

Urban legends are passed on from person to person and are a reflection of a particular culture. The twentieth century brought a new type of folktale that reflects a new urban culture. The urban legend is often an amusing story about something that could happen, but probably never really did. The person relating the story usually says it happened to the friend of a friend. It is a very memorable tale that is just a little difficult to believe. They are usually told in fun and reflect our need to be entertained by a story just a step beyond the ordinary. The following are examples of tales in circulation today:

◆ A set of twins—one boy and one girl—were born in a local hospital, and the mother explained to a friend that the social worker already named her children when she filled out the forms with the names "Molly" and "Femolly"—except the social worker spelled the names "m-a-l-e" and "f-e-m-a-l-e"!

◆ Stories abound about a thriving colony of white alligators that live in the sewers beneath New York City. They are said to be the offspring of baby alligators brought back from Florida as pets. One man claims to have done battle with several of them and barely surviving. The city fears the legendary creatures even though it is common knowledge that alligators could not possibly survive the cold temperatures of New York City.

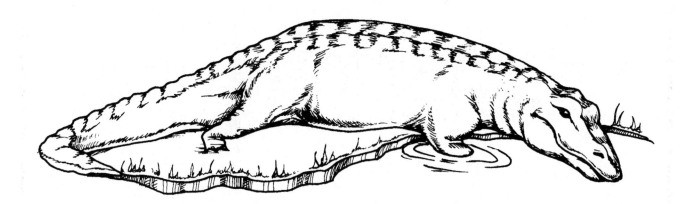

◆ A woman accidentally ran over her neighbor's cat. Thoughtfully, she put it in a paper bag to dispose of later. The bag was stolen by another woman, who then went to a restaurant. When that woman looked in the bag and saw the dead cat, she fainted and an ambulance was called. Believing it was the unconscious woman's valuable possession, a waitress from the restaurant carefully put the bag beside the thief on the stretcher!

Presentation Time: 1 to 3 minutes

Assignment: Relate to the class an urban legend you have heard. If you wish, you may be creative and create your own. Use the storyboard organizer on page 102 to help you plan your story.

Storytelling: Urban Legends *(cont.)*

Storyboard Organizer

Topic:_____

Characters	Action	Outcomes

Treasures from the Past

We are all where we are today because of the chain of events that connect us with our pasts. Most of us have family stories we would like to write down and preserve.

Presentation Time: 3 to 8 minutes

Assignment: Select a family member or friend and complete the following form with him or her to record a story to be preserved. Share the story with the class.

When did this occur? _____

Where did the story take place? _____

List the people involved: _____

_____

State the problem or problems the people were experiencing: _____

_____

List the sequence of the action:

1. _____

2. _____

3. _____

4. _____

Conclusion: _____

_____

_____

_____

Changes the action and conclusion brought about in the lives of the people involved: _____

_____

_____

Your opinion of what happened: _____

_____

Puppetry

One of the earliest forms of drama that is still popular today is puppetry. Before you can put on a puppet show, you have to make puppets to represent your characters. Follow the instructions on this page and the following page to create puppets of your own. Then, complete the assignment on the following page.

Sock Puppets

Materials

- old socks
- cardboard
- white glue
- newspaper
- rubber bands
- pieces of felt
- fabric scraps

- handkerchiefs, bandanas, scarves
- googly eyes
- markers, paint (tempera)
- cardboard tubes (from toilet paper and paper towels)
- scissors
- paper towels (plain white or tan in color)

You can make almost any kind of puppet from an old sock. Here's how to make a funny dragon:

1. Cut a circle about 4–6 inches (10–15 cm) in diameter out of cardboard and fold it in half.

2. Apply glue in a circle around the outer edge.

3. Push the circle into the sock, all the way to the end, with the glued edges facing the toe.

4. Push in the toe of the sock so it sticks to the glued circle and let dry. This will form the dragon's mouth.

5. Roll up two balls from newspaper, about one inch (2.54 cm) across, and push them into the heel of the sock. These will form the dragon's eyes.

6. Wrap rubber bands around the base of the newspaper balls to form eyes that stick up. Glue on googly eyes.

7. Cut felt scales and glue them on the dragon's back.

8. Cut a red tongue and put it in the dragon's mouth.

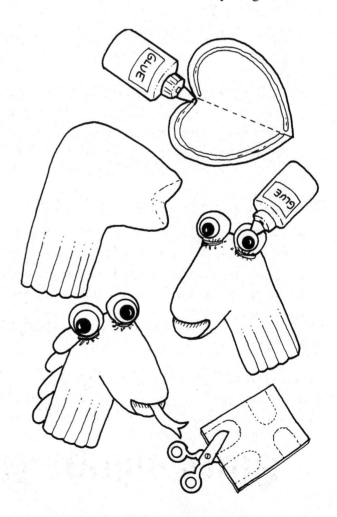

Puppetry *(cont.)*

Paper-Tube Puppets

Paper tubes are also good for making lots of different kinds of puppets. Here's how to make a wizard:

1. Cut a piece of cardboard tube about 2–3 inches (5–8 cm), depending on what you will make.

2. Tear a paper towel into pieces.

3. Mix together 3 tablespoons of white glue and 3 tablespoons of water.

4. Dip the paper towel pieces into the glue mixture and cover the outside of the tube with them.

5. Dip some more pieces of paper towel to make shapes like a nose and ears.

6. After it dries, use markers to draw the eyes, eyebrows, and mouth.

7. Out of cardboard, cut a cone-shaped hat, curl it into shape and tape it. Then glue it to the top of your wizard's head.

8. If you wish, you can decorate the hat with star stickers.

9. Drape a colorful handkerchief, bandana, or scarf over your hand. Put a rubber band around your little finger and the fabric and another rubber band around your thumb and the fabric. These will be the wizard's hands. Your middle three fingers, covered by fabric, go into the tube for the wizard's head.

To make a puppet stage:

1. Drape a sheet from a tabletop to the floor.

2. Puppeteers sit behind the table, hidden by the sheet.

3. Puppeteers raise hands to move puppets across the stage floor (tabletop).

4. Pin or attach stage decorations to the wall behind the table.

Presentation Time: 5 to 10 minutes

Assignment: Once you have a set and some puppets, it's time to write a puppet play. Form small groups and brainstorm for ideas. When presenting your puppet show, be sure to speak loudly and clearly when it is your puppet's turn to speak. You'll be hidden behind the stage so it will be more difficult than usual to hear you. Also, be sure to move your puppet when it is speaking.

Improvisations

This is a game of "Let's Pretend." Improvisation is similar to impromptu speaking in the fact that it is done on the spur of the moment with no preparation. Impromptu speaking is one speaker, but improvisation usually involves two or more actors creating a scene together. It is also similar to role playing, but role playing is usually used in conflict resolution and deals with understanding situations and motivations. Improvisation is usually a performance designed to entertain.

Presentation Time: 2 to 5 minutes

Assignment: Select partners, or just read the situation and participants may volunteer for the desired parts.

Two children trading comic books or trading cards

Friends discussing what they look for in a date

Friend trying to borrow a cell phone from another who was instructed not to make any more calls unless it was an emergency

Young child trying to give away kittens to loving homes

One teen trying to ask another out for a first date

Parent briefing child before the prom

Child selling cookies to several persons for school fundraiser

A marriage proposal

Person fries an egg on the sidewalk due to heat and is questioned by others

Son tells Dad he dented the car

Principal questions three students he/she suspects of throwing water balloons

Couple argues before the judge about who keeps the ring after the breakup

Young girls experiment with mom's makeup

Readers' Theater

Presentation Time: 15 minutes

An original script is included in this unit. It may be used as a classroom activity to provide opportunity to experience this type of theater.

Readers' theater is a communication form that establishes contact with the audience. In traditional drama, the audience is ignored and they watch as the characters react to the plot. Readers' theater observes the following characteristics:

1. The script is always read and never memorized.
2. Readers may be characters, narrators, or switch back and forth into various characters and parts.
3. The readers may sit, stand, or both, but they have no other actions.
4. Readers use only the interpreter's tools to express emotion. These are eye contact, facial expression, and vocal expression. The voice and vocal expression should be very expressive.
5. Scripts may contain quotations from songs, poems, letters, etc.
6. Musical accompaniment or soundtracks may be used.
7. If large segments of royalty plays and songs are used, permission must be obtained from the company if performed before an audience.
8. The production should always be very polished and well prepared.

Sleepy Tales

Cast of Characters			
Narrator 1 (N1)	Narrator 2(N3)	Narrator 3 (N2)	Narrator 4 (N4)

Narrators are seated on stools, with music stands in front of them to hold scripts. This may be presented on stage or as a classroom activity.

N1: For generations, the test of a really great story has been—
N2: Will it put us to sleep?
N3: Concern has grown over the amount of violence children experience today.
N4: Movies, videos, television, and even video games seem to be violent.
N1: So let us return to those healthy days of yesteryear.
N2: Perhaps the memories of these time-tested tales will cause your eyelids to grow heavy.
N3: Take care not to nod off as the classics bring back memories of being tucked in at bedtime.
N4: The tales we love to remember are filled with sweet little children who overcome odds.
N1: There are stories of bunny rabbits with cute names like Flopsy, Mopsy, and Cottontail.
N2: Stories of lovely ladies like Snow White, Cinderella, and Sleeping Beauty.
N3: All these wonderful characters had to face and overcome conflict.
N4: We learned bad things could happen to little bunnies who trespassed into gardens for carrot pie and discovered they might be the main dish!
N1: These stories became warnings to children of dangers lurking everywhere.
N2: (*Frightened*) One can never be too careful!
N3: So let us stroll back to "Once upon a time. . . ."
N4: In "Once upon a time . . ." there were many dangers.
N1: Danger sometimes took the form of tricky and deceitful wolves who pursued tender young ones.
N2: Ooh! Now I'm scared!

Readers' Theater *(cont.)*

Sleepy Tales *(cont.)*

N3: A wolf met Little Red Riding Hood when she was all alone in the deep, dark woods!

N4: Then he raced her to her kind, old grandmother's house and gobbled her grandma up like a Thanksgiving turkey!

N1: So much for non-violence. That would be rated R today!

N2: The wolf also was at the doors of the homes of each of the Three Pigs.

N3: He apparently was trick-or-treating for ham hocks and beans!

N4: Those might not be our most soothing stories—featuring carnivores and such! There were surely some vegetarians in some stories!

N1: Oh yes! Many stories feature conflict with environmental hazards.

N2: King Midas turned everything he touched to gold, including his child.

N3: Little Miss Muffet in the first production of *Arachnophobia*!

N4: Don't forget Alice who just accidentally stepped through the looking glass.

N1: Poor Jack and Jill met peril on a hill, which only goes to show that even hills may be hazardous to your health!

N2: The Three Bears family were forced to deal with breaking and entering, a serious crime in the inner-forest.

N3: Forget about the threats of loss of ozone! Chicken Little had to face the falling sky and the destruction of Earth as we know it!

N4: Don't forget Snow White eating a poisoned apple!

N1: Which brings us to the new threat that someone is out to get you!

N2: There was Rumplestiltskin, who tried to steal a baby.

N3: And the emperor who wanted to be a snazzy dresser—but paraded in the new see-through suit.

N4: There are many tales of witches and wicked stepmothers.

N1: Not much difference is drawn between the two.

N2: Cinderella and Snow White both had stepmothers who were not committed to the furthering of their careers.

N3: Hansel and Gretel were blessed with both a wicked stepmother who sent them into the woods to starve *and* a witch who wanted them for her Sunday buffet.

N4: We may conclude that stepmothers indeed may be hazardous to your health—and perhaps should be forced to wear a warning label.

N1: In hindsight, maybe our bedtime stories were not so innocent and soothing.

N2: These movies could never pass the ratings board today!

N3: We thought we'd relate to you—

N4: If we dare!

N1: The real source of your nightmares!

N2: Now I lay me down to sleep. . . .

N3: Sleep tight—your soul to keep.

N4: Just don't let the bedbugs bite!

All: (*In childish voices*) Could I please have a nightlight?

Melodrama

At the turn of the twentieth century, the melodrama became a very popular form of entertainment. It is still loved today and is one of the few entertainments that encourages audience participation. The following characteristics identify a story as a melodrama:

◆ The cast always includes a hero, heroine, and villain.

◆ Theme music is used to cue the entrance of the hero, heroine, and the villain. Classics such as "Strolling Through the Park" and "Hearts and Flowers" are good themes to cue the heroine. "Tie Her to the Tracks" is often used when the damsel is in distress.

◆ The story follows a formula: the villain pursues evil to win the heart of the heroine, but goodness and the hero conquer all.

◆ Melodrama is the art form that brought us fluttering eyelashes as a sign of flirtation. Both the heroine and the sign girl flirt with the audience. It adds to the production if they wear large, exaggerated eyelashes. They may be drawn on with eyeliner pencil.

◆ Sign girls strike different poses to hold the signs that signal the audience to cheer or boo.

◆ All acting is overdone, and gestures create a humorous effect. Language is stilted and overly dramatic. Actors speak directly to the audience and ham it up.

◆ Fights are very exaggerated and staged. Sometimes punches are accompanied by a drum beat.

◆ An *olio* often follows the production. This is a showcase to show the various talents of the cast. Characters may sing, tell jokes, dance, etc. This is the forerunner of the variety show, and many feel the olio was the inspiration for vaudeville.

Look for these characteristics of the melodrama as you and your classmates perform the play on pages 110 and 111. Remember, even if you're not playing one of the lead characters, you have the important part of being one of the townsfolk. It is your job to watch the sign girl and give the appropriate reaction to her signs.

Note: The sign girl will need large copies of the following signs:

Boo! Hiss!	**Cheer!**	**Aahhh!**

Midnight— The Next Evening	**The End**

Melodrama *(cont.)*

Dastardly Dealings at the Damsel's

or

Mend Your Cotton Pickin' Ways

<table>
<tr><td colspan="2" align="center">**Cast of Characters**</td></tr>
<tr><td>**Trudy Trueheart:** the heroine</td><td>**Gainly Goodguy:** the hero</td></tr>
<tr><td>**Widow Trueheart:** her mother</td><td>**Sign Girl**</td></tr>
<tr><td>**Dastardly Deathgrip:** the villain</td><td>**Townsfolk**</td></tr>
</table>

The set consists of a table with two chairs center stage. As the melodrama begins, Trudy and Widow Trueheart are seated at the table eating the evening meal. (Note: No other props are needed since all action will be pantomimed.)

Dastardly: (*Enters stage right and knocks at imaginary door*) Ya! Ha! Ha! (*Twirls imaginary cape and curls an imaginary mustache*)

Trudy: (*Rising and crossing right to door*) Who can that be at such a late hour? (*Tiptoes across the stage in exaggerated innocence*)

Dastardly: (*Villain theme may be played on tape recorder*) It is I, Dastardly Deathgrip!

Sign Girl: (*Enters right with Boo-Hiss! sign and strikes a pose*)

Dastardly: (*To audience*) Oh! Boo-hoo to you, too!

Trudy: Why, Mr. Deathgrip! How may I help you?

Dastardly: (*Kissing Trudy's hand*) My, how very lovely you look, Miss Trudy! I'm sure you know why I am here. Your dear father, God rest his soul, make a deal with the devil, so to speak!

Sign Girl: (*Enters with Boo-Hiss! sign*)

Dastardly: (*Waves off audience*) Your father was deeply in debt, and I so thoughtfully assisted him. He provided me with this deed to your cotton farm (*holds imaginary deed*). I'm afraid it is now time for me to collect and you and your dear mother, the Widow Trueheart, must vacate the premises by midnight tomorrow, according to the terms of your dear departed father's agreement. Do you have the money, my sweet Trudy?

Trudy: Indeed, I have told you I will not have the money. You must allow me more time. When our cotton crop comes in—we shall pay you every cent we owe!

Dastardly: No! No! I must remind you of the terms of our agreement. The debt will be forgiven and you and your dear mother may continue to reside here if you agree to become my wife! (*To audience*) The Mrs. Dastardly Deathgrip!

Sign Girl: (*Returns with Boo-Hiss! sign*)

Gainly Goodguy: (*Knocking at door-right*) Miss Trudy, is everything alright in there?

Sign Girl: (*Enters with Cheer! sign*)

Trudy: (*With hand at forehead*) No! No! A million times, no! I shall never marry you, Mr. Deathgrip! Alas, I shall be forced to vacate these premises to the nearest poor house and there reside with my honor intact!

Widow: (*Stands and crosses to Trudy*) Now let's not be too hasty! Perhaps a compromise may be reached! Perhaps you have another offer, Mr. Deathgrip?

Melodrama *(cont.)*

Dastardly: *(With a twirl of his cape he turns as if to go and encounters Gainly, who has entered through the open door)* That is my final offer! Take it or suffer the blows of fate!

Gainly: *(Grabs Dastardly by both shoulders. They rock and stomp with first downstage feet in unison and then upstage feet. Then they stomp back on downstage feet in a staged mock fight. Finally, Dastardly is thrown to stage right and exits.)* Dastardly, you shall not have your wicked ways with this fair damsel in distress! *(Forms a muscle with first the right arm and then the left)* Not as long as Gainly Goodguy resides in this territory!

Sign Girl: *(Enters with Cheer! sign)*

Trudy: *(Rushing to Gainly in adoration)* Oh! Gainly Goodguy! You are my true hero!

Sign Girl: *(Enters with Aah! sign)*

Widow: *(Rushes to Gainly's other side)* Oh Gainly! What can be done so we may continue to reside here in purity and in honor?

Trudy: *(Hand on forehead)* Alas! We have no money! Sorrowful was the day that my dear departed dad dealt that dastardly deal!

Gainly: But wait! I noticed on the way into your abode that you have a good cotton crop just standing in the field! It seemed that it—rather than you—was just ready for the picking! Perhaps I might enlist the aid of the simple townsfolk, and we may all join in to have a cotton-pickin' good time!

Sign Girl: *(Enters with Cheer! sign)*

Gainly: *(Flexes his muscles and exits stage right)*

Sign Girl: *(Holds up sign that says Midnight—the Next Evening)*

Dastardly: *(Music is played to signal villain. Knocks at door, stage right)* Trudy and the widow Trueheart. I have come for the decision! This is your day of reckoning! Shall it be me or your precious honor? *(Grabbing Trudy)* At last! You shall be my wife! Ya! Ha! Ha!

Sign Girl: *(Enters with Boo-hiss! sign)*

Trudy: *(Resisting Dastardly's advances)* No! No! A million times, no!

Townfolk: *(Enter from stage right)*

Gainly: *(Enters stage right with townsfolk—all say in unison)* Wait! We have the money!

Sign Girl: *(Enters with Cheer! sign)*

Gainly: These simple townsfolk have saved the day and Miss Trudy's honor! We have paid the debt in full in your bank account with the cotton picking funds! Now give me the deed, Dastardly! *(They struggle for the deed, and Gainly gets it.)*

Sign Girl: *(Enters with Cheer! sign)*

Dastardly: *(As he exits)* Curses! Foiled again!

Townfolk: *(Gather in a semi-circle behind main characters)*

Trudy: *(To Gainly)* My hero!

Sign Girl: *(Enters with Aah! sign)*

Gainly: *(Dropping to one knee)* Marry me, Trudy Trueheart!

Trudy: Yes! Yes! A million times yes!

Widow: And they lived happily ever after!

Sign Girl: *(Enters with Aah! sign, followed by Cheer! sign, followed by sign that reads The End.)* *(All bow.)*

Resources

Books

Bryant, Mary Helen. *Integrating Technology into the Curriculum.* Teacher Created Materials, Inc., 1996.

Dunbar, Robert E. *How to Debate.* Franklin Watts, 1994.

Ericson & Murphy. *Debater's Guide.* Southern Illinois University Press, 1987.

Espy, Willard. *A Children's Almanac of Words at Play.* Clarkson N. Patte, Inc., 1982.

Hayes, Deborah Shepherd. *Managing Technology in the Classroom.* Teacher Created Materials, Inc., 1995.

————. *Multimedia Projects.* Teacher Created Materials, Inc., 1997.

Jasmine, Julia. *Conflict Resolution.* Teacher Created Materials, Inc., 2000.

Johnson, Nancy. *Questioning Makes the Difference.* Pieces of Learning, 1990.

————. *Active Questioning.* Pieces of Learning, 1995.

————. *Quick Question Workbook.* Pieces of Learning, 1999.

Pereira, Linda. *Computers Don't Byte.* Teacher Created Materials, Inc., 1996.

Polette, Nancy. *Activities for Any Novel.* Pieces of Learning, 1999.

————. *U. S. History Readers Theatre.* Pieces of Learning, 1994.

Schwarta, Alvin. *Busy Buzzing Bumblebees.* Harper & Row, 1992.

Silverman, Janis. *Advanced Fairy Tales on Trial.* Pieces of Learning, 1999.

————. *Fairy Tales on Trail.* Pieces of Learning, 1999.

Smith, J. L. *Standards: Meeting Them in the Classroom.* Teacher Created Materials, 2000.

Software

Hyperstudio 3.0. Roger Wagner Publishing, Inc. 1050 Pioneer Way, Suite P., El Cajon, CA 92020. 1-800-421-6526.

Kid Pix 2. Broderbund Software Direct. P.O. Box 6125, Novato, CA 94948-6125. 1-800-474-8840.

Multimedia Workshop. Davidson and Associates. 19840 Pioneer Ave., Torrance, CA 90503. 1-800-545-7677.